The Britannica Guide to
Particle Physics

PHYSICS EXPLAINED

The Britannica Guide to
Particle Physics

EDITED BY ERIK GREGERSEN, ASSOCIATE EDITOR,
SCIENCE AND TECHNOLOGY

Britannica
Educational Publishing

IN ASSOCIATION WITH

ROSEN
EDUCATIONAL SERVICES

Published in 2011 by Britannica Educational Publishing
(a trademark of Encyclopædia Britannica, Inc.)
in association with Rosen Educational Services, LLC
29 East 21st Street, New York, NY 10010.

First Edition

Britannica Educational Publishing
Michael I. Levy: Executive Editor
J.E. Luebering: Senior Manager
Marilyn L. Barton: Senior Coordinator, Production Control
Steven Bosco: Director, Editorial Technologies
Lisa S. Braucher: Senior Producer and Data Editor
Yvette Charboneau: Senior Copy Editor
Kathy Nakamura: Manager, Media Acquisition
Erik Gregersen: Associate Editor, Science and Technology

Rosen Educational Services
Heather M. Moore Niver: Editor
Nelson Sá: Art Director
Cindy Reiman: Photography Manager
Matthew Cauli: Designer, Cover Design
Introduction by Erik Gregersen

Library of Congress Cataloging-in-Publication Data

The Britannica guide to particle physics / edited by Erik Gregersen.
    p. cm.—(Physics explained)
"In association with Britannica Educational Publishing, Rosen Educational Services."
Includes bibliographical references and index.
ISBN 978-1-61530-333-5 (lib. bdg.)
1. Particles (Nuclear physics)—Popular works. I. Gregersen, Erik. II. Title: Guide to particle physics. III. Title: Particle physics.
QC793.26.B75 2011
539.7'2—dc22

                                                                          2010030482

Manufactured in the United States of America

Cover, p. iii © www.istockphoto.com/Kasia Biel

On page x: One integral facet of particle physics is string theory, which considers particles more like "strings" than points, such as strings on a piano. *Bloomberg via Getty Images*

On page xviii: The Large Hadron Collider (model shown here) may help scientists understand the basic structure of matter. *Johannes Simon/Getty Images*

On pages 1, 49, 107, 165, 198, 204, 207, 211: The Milky Way Galaxy seems to be completely made up of matter, as scientists find no evidence of areas where matter and antimatter meet and extinguish. *NASA/CXC/UMass/D. Wang et al., NASA/ESA/STScI/D. Wang et al., NASA/JPL-Caltech/SSC/S.Stolovy*

CONTENTS

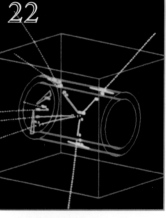

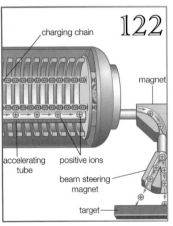

151

166

170

INTRODUCTION

Since English physicist J.J. Thomson discovered the electron over 100 years ago, understanding of what makes up the atom has revealed ever more interesting layers. This book in the Physics Explained series examines particle physics, the study of the astonishingly small subatomic particles that make up all matter.

The word "atom" comes from the Greek word *atomos* meaning indivisible. That is, according to ancient Greek philosophers such as Democritus and Leucippus, the atoms were the irreducible pieces of matter. The atoms had no internal ingredients or components. Because atoms were regarded as philosophical concepts, there was no idea of actually testing the irreducible nature of the atom. That had to wait until much later.

The first subatomic particle discovered was the electron in 1897. Physicist J.J. Thomson was investigating cathode rays. These were rays that were emitted from an electrode in a glass tube. Thomson did a series of three experiments. In the first two, he found that the cathode rays were particles that carried a negative electric charge. The smallest particles then known were atoms. So what kind of atom was the cathode ray? He then did another experiment that allowed him to measure the ratio of the cathode ray's mass to its charge. Much to everyone's surprise, the ratio was extremely small. So either the cathode ray has a very small mass, much smaller than that of any atom, or the cathode ray had an enormous charge, much more than had been seen on any atom. It turned out to be the former. Thomson called these little particles corpuscles, and they were later called electrons. The electron is the smallest of the famous three particles—protons, neutrons, and electrons—that make up atoms. It has a mass of 9.109×10^{-31} kg. If written out, there would be 30 zeros between the decimal point and the 9.

How the atom was actually constructed became clearer in 1911 when English physicist Ernest Rutherford posited that the atom was mostly empty space. There was a massive centre, and around it orbited the electrons. The atom was like the solar system in miniature, with the electrons as the planets. The centre was the nucleus, home to the larger protons and neutrons. The proton has a mass about 1,837 times that of the electron, which is still an extremely small mass.

However, even the proton and neutron could be divided further. Each of these two particles is made of quarks. Quarks are unusual particles that come in six flavours: up, down, top, bottom, charm, and strange. The proton is made up of two up quarks and one down. The neutron is one up and two down. The electron contained no quarks.

It was found that subatomic particles could be divided into two types: hadrons and leptons. The proton and neutron were hadrons (from the Greek for "heavy"); the electrons were leptons (from the Greek for "light"). The difference between the particles stems from how they relate to the fundamental forces. There are only four fundamental forces: gravity, electromagnetism, the weak force, and the strong force. The most well known is gravity. Gravity explains the apple falling out of the tree, the Moon orbiting Earth, and the galaxies interacting with each other. Because it works on the smallest scales of thousands of kilometres in the case of the apple and the largest scales of billions of light-years in the case of the galaxies, one might think that gravity was the strongest or the most "fundamental" force. It is actually the weakest. The distinction of being the strongest force belongs to the aptly named strong force, which binds the quarks together in hadrons. The leptons are not affected by the strong force.

The strong force is similar to electromagnetism in that the quarks carry a "charge." However, the charge is much more complicated than the simple positive and negative charges that drive electricity. The strong charge is called colour and comes in three types: red, green, and blue. Quarks of the same colour repel each other, while those with different colours attract. A hadron must be colour-neutral. The heavier, three-quark hadrons, or the baryons, have a red, a blue, and a green quark. The lighter, two-quark hadrons—or the mesons—consist of, for example, a red quark and antiquark, which has the colour of antired. Therefore the mesons are colour-neutral. The four forces have a carrier particle that transmits the force. In the case of the strong force, that particle is called the gluon. The theory that describes how colour works is called quantum chromodynamics.

Quantum chromodynamics, or QCD, is one of two theories that make up the Standard Model of particle physics. The other is electroweak theory, which describes electromagnetism and the weak force. Electromagnetism, like gravity, is a long-range force. The photons are the carrier particles of electromagnetism and can be seen across the universe. The weak force works in radioactive decay and thus works on the much smaller scales of the atomic nucleus. That these two vastly different forces can be described by one theory was one of the high points of particle physics.

The Standard Model is two theories joined together: QCD for the strong force and electroweak for electromagnetism and the weak force. Although particle physicists seek a grand unified theory that would describe all three forces, progress has been slow. Some promising grand unified theories predicted that the proton would decay after 10^{32} years. These theories could be easily tested. Several thousand tons of water contain about 10^{33} protons. Several experiments have placed huge tanks deep underground to be shielded from cosmic radiation that would look like a proton decay. No proton decays have been seen. However, different theories suggest that current experiments are not sensitive enough to detect proton decays. That is, the proton decay time is longer than 10^{33} years, and thus bigger tanks would be needed.

Many early particle physics experiments were performed using radioactive elements, which are more complicated than several thousand tons of water but much more portable. Atoms in the element decayed emitting some particle. However, the energy that is released in natural radioactivity is limited. To study particles at higher energies, they needed to be accelerated. Beginning in the 1930s, apparatuses were built that did just that. The first particle accelerators were quite small. In 1931 Ernest O. Lawrence built the first cyclotron, which was about 11 cm (4.5 inches) across. The particle accelerator soon got off the tabletop in the lab and by the 1950s needed its own building. By the 1960s, it had escaped the building, too. The Stanford Linear Accelerator Center (SLAC) had a linear accelerator 3.2 km (2 miles) long. The synchrotron at the Fermi National Accelerator Laboratory had a circumference of 6.3 km (3.9 miles). In the late 1980s construction began in Texas on the Superconducting Super Collider, which was designed with a 87-km (54-mile) circumference. However, the project was canceled in 1993 when funding was no longer available.

One of the most recent developments in the field of particle physics has been the activation of the Large Hadron Collider (LHC) underneath the border between the countries of France and Switzerland. The LHC is one of the largest scientific projects ever, occupying a 27-km (17-mile) tunnel. It will take protons and collide them together with such high energies that the protons will break down, leaving the quarks floating in a quark-gluon plasma. These were the conditions shortly after the beginning of the universe, specifically 10^{-25} second after the Big Bang. At that time, the universe had a radius of 300 million km (200 million miles) and would have fit comfortably inside the asteroid belt of the modern solar system. The energy achieved by the protons increases with the radius of particle accelerator. There will probably never be built an accelerator larger than the LHC. This immense and complex one-of-a-kind machine is not expected to be fully operational until 2013. However, even operating at its limited capacity, it is still the most powerful particle accelerator on the planet.

The LHC should be able to solve many of the fundamental problems of particle physics. For example, the origin of mass is unknown. Why are some particles heavier than others? It has been speculated that there is a field (named after British physicist Peter Higgs) that has a carrier particle, the Higgs boson. The Higgs boson has not been seen yet, but there is an upper limit to its mass. That limit is well within the capabilities of the LHC.

Another problem that could be solved by the LHC is the nature of dark matter. Most of the matter in the universe can only be seen through its gravitational influence. In studying galaxies, one can take the amount of light and thus get a good idea of how many stars there are in the galaxy and therefore how much mass the stars in a galaxy have. However, one can measure the speed with which star orbits in the galaxy and thus how much matter the star is orbiting. In quite a few galaxies, the speed of the stars shows much more matter than is shown by the starlight. That is, the light coming from the stars only comes from a portion of the matter. This matter is some kind of particle that only interacts with other matter through gravity. This hypothetical particle is a WIMP, a weakly interacting massive particle. Perhaps the WIMPs may be produced at the LHC.

Another startling development in particle physics has been the arrival of string theory. In this description of the universe, particles are strings. These strings are very small with lengths of about 10^{-33} cm. The mass and charge of a particle are determined by the vibration of the string. One could even analogize particles to music, with some particles being the normal mode and others being different because they vibrate at different frequencies. String theory also posits six extra spatial dimensions. The reason no one experiences spatial dimensions four through nine is that they are rolled up. The common description is that we are like ants on a wire. The ant crawls forward and backward. It is confined to one dimension. The wire does have some thickness, but because the thickness is small, the ant does not really experience the second and third dimension. In string theory, the extra dimensions are "rolled up" like the wire and thus have an exceptionally small thickness. If these extra dimensions exist, the LHC could detect them.

The LHC may find the Higgs boson. It may find extra dimensions of space. Or it may find the WIMP that is spread throughout the galaxies. Whatever the results from the LHC, the discoveries there will build upon the particle physics described in this book.

CHAPTER 1
BASIC CONCEPTS OF PARTICLE PHYSICS

S ubatomic, or elementary, particles are various self-contained units of matter or energy that are the fundamental constituents of all matter. They include electrons, the negatively charged, almost massless particles that nevertheless account for most of the size of the atom, and they include the heavier building blocks of the small but very dense nucleus of the atom, the positively charged protons and the electrically neutral neutrons. But these basic atomic components are by no means the only known subatomic particles. Protons and neutrons, for instance, are themselves made up of elementary particles called quarks, and the electron is only one member of a class of elementary particles that also includes the muon and the neutrino. More unusual subatomic particles— such as the positron, the antimatter counterpart of the electron—have been detected and characterized in cosmic-ray interactions in the Earth's atmosphere. The field of subatomic particles has expanded dramatically with the construction of powerful particle accelerators to study high-energy collisions of electrons, protons, and other particles with matter. As particles collide at high energy, the collision energy becomes available for the creation of subatomic particles such as mesons and hyperons. Finally, completing the revolution that began in the early 20th century with theories of the equivalence of matter and energy, the study of subatomic particles has been transformed by the discovery that the actions of forces are due to the exchange of "force" particles such as photons and gluons. More than 200 subatomic particles have been detected—most of them highly unstable, existing for less than a millionth of a second—as a result of collisions produced in cosmic-ray reactions or particle-accelerator experiments. Theoretical and experimental research in particle physics, the study of subatomic particles and their properties, has given scientists a clearer understanding of the nature of matter and energy and of the origin of the universe.

The current understanding of the state of particle physics is integrated within a conceptual framework known as the Standard Model. The Standard Model provides a classification scheme for all the known subatomic particles based on theoretical descriptions of the basic forces of matter.

THE DIVISIBLE ATOM

The physical study of subatomic particles became possible only during the 20th century, with the development of increasingly sophisticated apparatuses to probe matter at scales of 10^{-15} metre and less (that is, at distances comparable to the diameter of the proton or neutron). Yet the basic philosophy of the subject now known as particle physics dates to at least 500 BCE, when the Greek philosopher Leucippus and his pupil Democritus put forward the notion that matter consists of invisibly small, indivisible particles, which they called atoms. For more than 2,000 years the idea of atoms lay largely neglected, while the opposing view that matter consists of four elements— earth, fire, air, and water—held sway. But by the beginning of the 19th century, the atomic theory of matter had returned to favour, strengthened in particular by the work of John Dalton, an English chemist whose studies suggested that each chemical element consists of its own unique kind of atom. As such, Dalton's atoms are still the atoms of modern physics. By the close of the century, however, the first indications began to emerge that atoms are not indivisible, as Leucippus and Democritus had imagined, but that they instead contain smaller particles.

In 1896 the French physicist Henri Becquerel discovered radioactivity, and in the following year J.J. Thomson, a professor of physics at the University of Cambridge in England, demonstrated the existence of tiny particles much smaller in mass than hydrogen, the lightest atom. Thomson had discovered the first subatomic particle, the electron. Six years later Ernest Rutherford and Frederick Soddy, working at McGill University in Montreal, found that radioactivity occurs when atoms of one type transmute into those of another kind. The idea of atoms as immutable, indivisible objects had become untenable.

The basic structure of the atom became apparent in 1911, when Rutherford showed that most of the mass of an atom lies concentrated at its centre, in a tiny nucleus. Rutherford postulated that the atom resembled a miniature solar system, with light, negatively charged electrons orbiting the dense, positively charged nucleus, just as the planets orbit the Sun. The Danish theorist Niels Bohr refined this model in 1913 by incorporating the new ideas of quantization that had been developed by the German physicist Max Planck at the turn of the century. Planck had theorized that electromagnetic radiation, such as light, occurs in discrete bundles, or "quanta," of energy now known as photons. Bohr postulated that electrons circled the nucleus in orbits of fixed size and energy and that an electron could jump from one orbit to another only by emitting or absorbing specific quanta of energy. By thus incorporating quantization into his theory of the atom, Bohr introduced one of the basic elements of modern particle physics and prompted wider acceptance of quantization to explain atomic and subatomic phenomena.

SIZE

Subatomic particles play two vital roles in the structure of matter. They are both the basic building blocks of the universe and the mortar that binds the blocks. Although the particles that fulfill these different roles are of two distinct types, they do share some common characteristics, foremost of which is size.

The small size of subatomic particles is perhaps most convincingly expressed not by stating their absolute units of measure but by comparing them with the complex particles of which they are a part. An atom, for instance, is typically 10^{-10} metre across, yet almost all of the size of the atom is unoccupied "empty" space available to the point-charge electrons surrounding the nucleus. The distance across an atomic nucleus of average size is roughly 10^{-14} metre—only $\frac{1}{10,000}$ the diameter of the atom. The nucleus, in turn, is made up of positively charged protons and electrically neutral neutrons, collectively referred to as nucleons, and a single nucleon has a diameter of about 10^{-15} metre—that is, about $\frac{1}{10}$ that of the nucleus and $\frac{1}{100,000}$ that of the atom. (The distance across the nucleon, 10^{-15} metre, is known as a *fermi*, in honour of the Italian-born physicist Enrico Fermi, who did much experimental and theoretical work on the nature of the nucleus and its contents.)

The sizes of atoms, nuclei, and nucleons are measured by firing a beam of electrons at an appropriate target. The higher the energy of the electrons, the farther they penetrate before being deflected by the electric charges within the atom. For example, a beam with an energy of a few hundred electron volts (eV) scatters from the electrons in a target atom. The way in which the beam is scattered (electron scattering) can then be studied to determine the general distribution of the atomic electrons.

At energies of a few hundred megaelectron volts (MeV; 10^6 eV), electrons in the beam are little affected by atomic electrons. Instead, they penetrate the atom and are scattered by the positive nucleus. Therefore, if such a beam is fired at liquid hydrogen, whose atoms contain only single protons in their nuclei, the pattern of scattered electrons reveals the size of the proton. At energies greater than a gigaelectron volt (GeV; 10^9 eV), the electrons penetrate within the protons and neutrons, and their scattering patterns reveal an inner structure. Thus, protons and neutrons are no more indivisible than atoms are. Indeed, they contain still smaller particles, which are called quarks.

Quarks are as small as or smaller than physicists can measure. In experiments at very high energies, equivalent to probing protons in a target with electrons accelerated to nearly 50,000 GeV, quarks appear to behave as points in space, with no measurable size. They must therefore be smaller than 10^{-18} metre, or less than $\frac{1}{1,000}$ the size of the individual nucleons they form. Similar experiments show that electrons too are smaller than it is possible to measure.

ELEMENTARY PARTICLES

Electrons and quarks contain no discernible structure. They cannot be reduced or separated into smaller components. It is therefore reasonable to call them "elementary" particles, a name that in the past was mistakenly given to particles such as the proton, which is in fact a complex particle that contains quarks. The term *subatomic particle* refers both to the true elementary particles, such as quarks and electrons, and to the larger particles that quarks form.

Although both are elementary particles, electrons and quarks differ in several respects. Whereas quarks together form nucleons within the atomic nucleus, the electrons generally circulate toward the periphery of atoms.

Indeed, electrons are regarded as distinct from quarks and are classified in a separate group of elementary particles called leptons. There are several types of lepton, just as there are several types of quark. Only two types of quark are needed to form protons and neutrons, however, and these, together with the electron and one other elementary particle, are all the building blocks that are necessary to build the everyday world. The last particle required is an electrically neutral particle called the neutrino.

Neutrinos do not exist within atoms in the sense that electrons do, but they play a crucial role in certain types of radioactive decay. In a basic process of one type of radioactivity, known as beta decay, a neutron changes into a proton. In making this change, the neutron acquires one unit of positive charge. To keep the overall charge in the beta-decay process constant and thereby conform to the fundamental physical law of charge conservation, the neutron must emit a negatively charged electron. In addition, the neutron also emits a neutrino (strictly speaking, an antineutrino), which has little or no mass and no electric charge. Beta decays are important in the transitions that occur when unstable atomic nuclei change to become more stable, and for this reason neutrinos are a necessary component in establishing the nature of matter.

The neutrino, like the electron, is classified as a lepton. Thus, it seems at first sight that only four kinds of elementary particles—two quarks and two leptons—should exist. In the 1930s, however, long before the concept of quarks was established, it became clear that matter is more complicated.

SPIN

The concept of quantization led during the 1920s to the development of quantum mechanics, which appeared to provide physicists with the correct method of calculating the structure of the atom. In his model, Niels Bohr had postulated that the electrons in the atom move only in orbits in which the angular momentum (angular velocity multiplied by mass) has certain fixed values. Each of these allowed values is characterized by a quantum number that can have only integer values. In the full quantum mechanical treatment of the structure of the atom, developed in the 1920s, three quantum numbers relating to angular momentum arise because there are three independent variable parameters in the equation describing the motion of atomic electrons.

In 1925, however, two Dutch physicists, Samuel Goudsmit and George Uhlenbeck, realized that, to explain fully the spectra of light emitted by the atoms of alkali metals, such as sodium, which have one outer valence electron beyond the main core, there must be a fourth quantum number that can take only two values, -½ and +½. Goudsmit and Uhlenbeck proposed that this quantum number refers to an internal angular momentum, or spin, that the electrons possess. This implies that the electrons, in effect, behave like spinning electric charges. Each therefore creates a magnetic field and has its own magnetic moment. The internal magnet of an atomic electron orients itself in one of two directions with respect to the magnetic field created by the rest of the atom. It is either parallel or antiparallel. Hence, there are two quantized states—and two possible values of the associated spin quantum number.

The concept of spin is now recognized as an intrinsic property of all subatomic particles. Indeed, spin is one of the key criteria used to classify particles into two main groups: fermions, with half-integer values of spin ($\frac{1}{2}$, $\frac{3}{2}$, ...), and bosons, with integer values of spin (0, 1, 2, ...). In the Standard Model all of the "matter" particles (quarks and leptons) are fermions, whereas "force" particles such as photons are bosons. These two classes of particles have different symmetry properties that affect their behaviour.

ANTIPARTICLES

Two years after the work of Goudsmit and Uhlenbeck, the English theorist P.A.M. Dirac provided a sound theoretical background for the concept of electron spin. To describe the behaviour of an electron in an electromagnetic field, Dirac introduced the German-born physicist Albert Einstein's theory of special relativity into quantum mechanics. Dirac's relativistic theory showed that the electron must have spin and a magnetic moment, but it also made what seemed a strange prediction. The basic equation describing the allowed energies for an electron would admit two solutions, one positive and one negative. The positive solution apparently described normal electrons. The negative solution was more of a mystery. It seemed to describe electrons with positive rather than negative charge.

The mystery was resolved in 1932, when Carl Anderson, an American physicist, discovered the particle called the positron. Positrons are very much like electrons: they have the same mass and the same spin, but they have opposite electric charge. Positrons, then, are the particles predicted by Dirac's theory, and they were the first of the so-called antiparticles to be discovered. Dirac's theory, in fact, applies to any subatomic particle with spin ½. Therefore, all spin-½ particles should have corresponding antiparticles. Matter cannot be built from both particles and antiparticles, however. When a particle meets its appropriate antiparticle, the two disappear in an act of mutual destruction known as annihilation. Atoms can exist only because there is an excess of electrons, protons, and neutrons in the everyday world, with no corresponding positrons, antiprotons, and antineutrons.

Positrons do occur naturally, however, which is how Anderson discovered their existence. High-energy subatomic particles in the form of cosmic rays continually rain down on the Earth's atmosphere from outer space, colliding with atomic nuclei and generating showers of particles that cascade toward the ground. In these showers the enormous energy of the incoming cosmic ray is converted to matter,

Electrons and positrons produced simultaneously from individual gamma rays curl in opposite directions in the magnetic field of a bubble chamber. Here the gamma ray has lost some energy to an atomic electron, which leaves the long track, curling left. The gamma rays do not leave tracks in the chamber, because they have no electric charge. Courtesy of the Lawrence Berkeley Laboratory

in accordance with Einstein's theory of special relativity, which states that $E = mc^2$, where E is energy, m is mass, and c is the velocity of light. Among the particles created are pairs of electrons and positrons. The positrons survive for a tiny fraction of a second until they come close enough to electrons to annihilate. The total mass of each electron-positron pair is then converted to energy in the form of gamma-ray photons.

Using particle accelerators, physicists can mimic the action of cosmic rays and create collisions at high energy.

In 1955 a team led by the Italian-born scientist Emilio Segrè and the American Owen Chamberlain found the first evidence for the existence of antiprotons in collisions of high-energy protons produced by the Bevatron, an accelerator at what is now the Lawrence Berkeley National Laboratory in California. Shortly afterward, a different team working on the same accelerator discovered the antineutron.

Since the 1960s physicists have discovered that protons and neutrons consist of quarks with spin ½ and that antiprotons and antineutrons consist of antiquarks. Neutrinos too have spin ½ and therefore have corresponding antiparticles known as antineutrinos. Indeed, it is an antineutrino, rather than a neutrino, that emerges when a neutron changes by beta decay into a proton. This reflects an empirical law regarding the production and decay of quarks and leptons: in any interaction the total numbers of quarks and leptons seem always to remain constant. Thus, the appearance of a lepton—the electron—in the decay of a neutron must be balanced by the simultaneous appearance of an antilepton, in this case the antineutrino.

More than 200 subatomic particles have been discovered. All these particles are now known to have corresponding antiparticles. Thus, there are positive and negative muons, positive and negative pi-mesons, and the K-meson and the anti-K-meson, plus a long list of baryons and antibaryons. Most of these newly discovered particles have too short a lifetime to be able to combine with electrons. The exception is the positive muon, which, together with an electron, has been observed to form a muonium atom.

These more than 200 "extra" particles do not appear in the low-energy environment of everyday human experience. They emerge only at the higher energies found in cosmic rays or particle accelerators. Moreover, they immediately decay to the more familiar particles after brief lifetimes of only fractions of a second. The variety and behaviour of these extra particles initially bewildered scientists but have since come to be understood in terms of the quarks and leptons. In fact, only six quarks, six leptons, and their corresponding antiparticles are necessary to explain the variety and behaviour of all the subatomic particles, including those that form normal atomic matter.

The Dirac theory also predicts that an electron and a positron, because of Coulomb attraction of their opposite charges, will combine to form an intermediate bound state, just as an electron and a proton combine to form a hydrogen atom. The e^+e^- bound system is called positronium. The annihilation of positronium into gamma rays has been observed. Its measured lifetime depends on the orientation of the two particles and is on the order of 10^{-10}–10^{-7} second, in agreement with that computed from Dirac's theory.

In 1995 physicists at the European Organization for Nuclear Research (CERN) in Geneva created the first antiatom, the antimatter counterpart of an ordinary atom—in this case, antihydrogen, the simplest antiatom, consisting of a positron in orbit around an antiproton nucleus. They did so by firing antiprotons through a xenon-gas jet. In the strong electric fields surrounding the xenon nuclei, some antiprotons created pairs of electrons and positrons. A few of the positrons thus produced then combined with the antiprotons to form antihydrogen. Each antiatom survived for only about forty-billionths of a second before it came into contact with ordinary matter and was annihilated. CERN plans to produce larger amounts of antihydrogen to study the spectrum of the antihydrogen atom. A comparison with the well-studied spectrum of hydrogen could reveal small differences between matter and antimatter, which would have important implications for theories of how matter formed in the early universe.

Although positrons are readily created in the collisions of cosmic rays, there is no evidence for the existence of large amounts of antimatter in the universe. The Milky Way Galaxy appears to consist entirely of matter, as there are no indications for regions where matter and antimatter meet and annihilate to produce characteristic gamma rays. The implication that matter completely dominates antimatter in the universe appears to be in contradiction to Dirac's theory, which, supported by experiment, shows that particles and antiparticles are always created in equal numbers from energy. The energetic conditions of the early universe should have created equal numbers of particles and antiparticles. Mutual annihilation of particle-antiparticle pairs, however, would have left nothing but energy. In the universe today, photons (energy) outnumber protons (matter) by a factor of one billion. This suggests that most of the particles created in the early universe were indeed annihilated by antiparticles, while one in a billion particles had no matching antiparticle and so survived to form the matter observed today in stars and galaxies. The tiny imbalance between particles and antiparticles in the early universe is referred to as matter-antimatter asymmetry, and its cause remains a major unsolved puzzle for cosmology and particle physics. One possible explanation is that it involves a phenomenon known as CP violation, which gives rise to a small but significant difference in the behaviour of particles called K-mesons and their antiparticles.

FOUR BASIC FORCES

Quarks and leptons are the building blocks of matter, but they require some sort of mortar to bind themselves together into more complex forms, whether on a nuclear or a universal scale. The particles that provide this mortar are associated with four basic forces that are collectively referred to as the fundamental interactions of matter. These four basic forces are gravity (or the gravitational force), the electromagnetic force, and two forces more familiar to physicists than to laypeople: the strong force and the weak force.

On the largest scales the dominant force is gravity. Gravity governs the aggregation of matter into stars and galaxies and influences the way that the universe has evolved since its origin in the big bang. The best-understood force, however, is the electromagnetic force, which underlies the related phenomena of electricity and magnetism. The electromagnetic force binds negatively charged electrons to positively charged atomic nuclei and gives rise to the bonding between atoms to form matter in bulk.

Gravity and electromagnetism are well known at the macroscopic level. The other two forces act only on subatomic scales, indeed on subnuclear scales. The strong force binds quarks together within protons, neutrons, and other subatomic particles. Rather as the electromagnetic force is ultimately responsible for holding bulk matter together, so the strong force also keeps protons and neutrons together within atomic nuclei. Unlike the strong force, which acts only between quarks, the weak force acts on both quarks and leptons. This force is responsible for the beta decay of a neutron into a proton and for the nuclear reactions that fuel the Sun and other stars.

FIELD THEORY

Since the 1930s physicists have recognized that they can use field theory to describe the interactions of all four basic forces with matter. In mathematical terms a field describes something that varies continuously through space and time. A familiar example is the field that surrounds a piece of magnetized iron. The magnetic field maps the way that the force varies in strength and direction around the magnet. The appropriate fields for the four basic forces appear to have an important property in common: they all exhibit what is known as gauge symmetry. Put simply, this means that certain changes can be made that do not affect the basic structure of the field. It also implies that the relevant physical laws are the same in different regions of space and time.

At a subatomic, quantum level these field theories display a significant feature. They describe each basic force as being in a sense carried by its own subatomic particles. These "force" particles are now called gauge bosons, and they differ from the "matter" particles—the quarks and leptons discussed earlier—in a fundamental way. Bosons are characterized by integer values of their spin quantum number, whereas quarks and leptons have half-integer values of spin.

The most familiar gauge boson is the photon, which transmits the electromagnetic force between electrically charged objects such as electrons and protons. The photon acts as a private, invisible messenger between these particles, influencing their behaviour with the information it conveys, rather as a ball influences the actions of children playing catch. Other gauge bosons, with varying properties, are involved with the other basic forces.

In developing a gauge theory for the weak force in the 1960s, physicists discovered that the best theory, which would always yield sensible answers, must also incorporate the electromagnetic force. The result was what is now called electroweak theory. It was the first workable example of a unified field theory linking forces that manifest themselves differently in the everyday world. Unified theory reveals that the basic forces, though outwardly diverse, are in fact separate facets of a single underlying force. The search for a unified theory of everything, which incorporates all four fundamental forces, is one of the major goals of particle physics. It is leading theorists to an exciting area of study that involves not only subatomic particle physics but also cosmology and astrophysics.

THE BASIC FORCES AND THEIR MESSENGER PARTICLES

There are four fundamental interactions, or basic forces, that affect all of matter. Each force is described on the basis of the following characteristics: (1) the property of matter on which each force acts; (2) the particles of matter that experience the force; (3) the nature of the messenger particle (gauge boson) that mediates the force; and (4) the relative strength and range of the force.

GRAVITY

The weakest, and yet the most pervasive, of the four basic forces is gravity. It acts on all forms of mass and energy and thus acts on all subatomic particles, including the gauge bosons that carry the forces. The 17th-century English scientist Isaac Newton was the first to develop a quantitative description of the force of gravity. He argued that the force that binds the Moon in orbit around the Earth is the same force that makes apples and other objects fall to the ground, and he proposed a universal law of gravitation.

According to Newton's law, all bodies are attracted to each other by a force that depends directly on the mass of each body and inversely on the square of the distance between them. For a pair of masses, m_1 and m_2, a distance r apart, the strength of the force F is given by $F = Gm_1m_2/r^2$. G is called the constant of gravitation and is equal to 6.67×10^{-11} newton-metre^2-kilogram^{-2}.

The constant G gives a measure of the strength of the gravitational force, and its smallness indicates that gravity is weak. Indeed, on the scale of atoms the effects of gravity are negligible compared with the other forces at work. Although the gravitational force is weak, its effects can be extremely long-ranging. Newton's law shows that at some distance the gravitational force between two bodies becomes negligible but that this distance depends on the masses involved. Thus, the gravitational effects of large, massive objects can be considerable, even at distances far outside the range of the other forces. The gravitational force of the Earth, for example, keeps the Moon in orbit some 384,400 km (238,900 miles) distant.

Newton's theory of gravity proves adequate for many applications. In 1915, however, the German-born physicist Albert Einstein developed the theory of general relativity, which incorporates the concept of gauge symmetry and yields subtle corrections to Newtonian gravity. Despite its importance, Einstein's general relativity remains a classical theory in the sense that it does not incorporate the ideas of quantum mechanics. In a quantum theory of gravity, the gravitational force must be carried by a suitable messenger particle, or gauge boson. No workable quantum theory of gravity has yet been developed, but general relativity determines some of the properties of the hypothesized "force" particle of gravity, the so-called graviton. In particular, the graviton must have a spin quantum number of 2 and no mass, only energy.

ELECTROMAGNETISM

The first proper understanding of the electromagnetic force dates to the 18th century, when a French physicist, Charles Coulomb, showed that the electrostatic force between electrically charged objects follows a law similar to Newton's law of gravitation. According to Coulomb's law, the force F between one charge, q_1, and a second charge, q_2, is proportional to the product of the charges divided by the square of the distance r between them, or $F = kq_1q_2/r^2$. Here k is the proportionality constant, equal to $\frac{1}{4}\pi\varepsilon_0$ (ε_0 being the permittivity of free space). An electrostatic force can be either attractive or repulsive, because the source of the force, electric charge, exists in opposite forms: positive and negative. The force between opposite charges is attractive, whereas bodies with the same kind of charge experience a repulsive force. Coulomb also showed that the force between magnetized bodies varies inversely as the square of the distance between them. Again, the force can be attractive (opposite poles) or repulsive (like poles).

Magnetism and electricity are not separate phenomena. They are the related manifestations of an underlying electromagnetic force. Experiments in the early 19th century by, among others, Hans Ørsted (in Denmark), André-Marie Ampère (in France), and Michael Faraday (in England) revealed the intimate connection between electricity and magnetism and the way the one can give rise to the other. The results of these experiments were synthesized in the 1850s by the Scottish physicist James Clerk Maxwell in his electromagnetic theory. Maxwell's theory predicted the existence of electromagnetic waves—undulations in intertwined electric and magnetic fields, traveling with the velocity of light.

Max Planck's work in Germany at the turn of the 20th century, in which he explained the spectrum of radiation from a perfect emitter (blackbody radiation), led to the concept of quantization and photons. In the quantum picture, electromagnetic radiation has a dual nature, existing both as Maxwell's waves and as streams of photons. The quantum nature of electromagnetic radiation is encapsulated in quantum electrodynamics, the quantum field theory of the electromagnetic force. Both Maxwell's classical theory and the quantized version contain gauge symmetry, which now appears to be a basic feature of the fundamental forces.

The electromagnetic force is intrinsically much stronger than the gravitational force. If the relative strength of the electromagnetic force between two protons separated by the distance within the nucleus was set equal to one, the strength of the gravitational force would be only 10^{-36}. At an atomic level the electromagnetic force is almost completely in control. Gravity dominates on a large scale only because matter as a whole is electrically neutral.

The gauge boson of electromagnetism is the photon, which has zero mass and a spin quantum number of 1. Photons are exchanged whenever electrically charged subatomic particles interact. The photon has no electric charge, so it does not experience the electromagnetic force itself. In other words, photons cannot interact directly with one another. Photons do carry energy and

momentum, however, and, in transmitting these properties between particles, they produce the effects known as
electromagnetism.

In these processes energy and momentum are conserved overall (that is, the totals remain the same, in
accordance with the basic laws of physics), but, at the
instant one particle emits a photon and another particle
absorbs it, energy is not conserved. Quantum mechanics
allows this imbalance, provided that the photon fulfills
the conditions of Heisenberg's uncertainty principle.
This rule, described in 1927 by the German scientist
Werner Heisenberg, states that it is impossible, even
in principle, to know all the details about a particular
quantum system. For example, if the exact position of
an electron is identified, it is impossible to be certain of
the electron's momentum. This fundamental uncertainty
allows a discrepancy in energy, ΔE, to exist for a time,
Δt, provided that the product of ΔE and Δt is extremely
small—equal to the value of Planck's constant divided
by 2π, or 1.05×10^{-34} joule seconds. The energy of the
exchanged photon can thus be thought of as "borrowed,"
within the limits of the uncertainty principle (i.e., the
more energy borrowed, the shorter the time of the loan).
Such borrowed photons are called "virtual" photons to
distinguish them from real photons, which constitute
electromagnetic radiation and can, in principle, exist forever. This concept of virtual particles in processes that
fulfill the conditions of the uncertainty principle applies
to the exchange of other gauge bosons as well.

THE WEAK FORCE

Since the 1930s physicists have been aware of a force
within the atomic nucleus that is responsible for certain

types of radioactivity that are classed together as beta decay. A typical example of beta decay occurs when a neutron transmutes into a proton. The force that underlies this process is known as the weak force to distinguish it from the strong force that binds quarks together. The weak force acts upon all known fermions.

Most subatomic particles are unstable and decay by the weak force, even if they cannot decay by the electromagnetic force or the strong force. The lifetimes for particles that decay via the weak force vary from as little as 10^{-13} second to 896 seconds, the mean life of the free neutron. Neutrons bound in atomic nuclei can be stable, as they are when they occur in the familiar chemical elements, but they can also give rise through weak decays to the type of radioactivity known as beta decay. In this case the lifetimes of the nuclei can vary from a thousandth of a second to millions of years. Although low-energy weak interactions are feeble, they occur frequently at the heart of the Sun and other stars where both the temperature and the density of matter are high. In the nuclear-fusion process that is the source of stellar-energy production, two protons interact via the weak force to form a deuterium nucleus, which reacts further to generate helium with the concomitant release of large amounts of energy.

The correct gauge field theory for the weak force incorporates the quantum field theory of electromagnetism (quantum electrodynamics) and is called electroweak theory. It treats the weak force and the electromagnetic force on an equal footing by regarding them as different manifestations of a more-fundamental electroweak force, rather as electricity and magnetism appear as different aspects of the electromagnetic force.

The electroweak theory requires four gauge bosons. One of these is the photon of electromagnetism. The other three are involved in reactions that occur via the weak force. These weak gauge bosons include two electrically charged versions, called W^+ and W^-, where the signs indicate the charge, and a neutral variety called Z°, where the zero indicates no charge. Like the photon, the W and Z particles have a spin quantum number of 1. Unlike the photon, they are rather massive. The W particles have a mass of about 80.4 GeV, while the mass of the Z° particle is 91.187 GeV. By comparison, the mass of the proton is 0.94 GeV, or about $\frac{1}{100}$ that of the Z particle. (Strictly speaking, mass should be given in units of energy/c^2, where c is the velocity of light. However, common practice is to set $c = 1$ so that mass is quoted simply in units of energy, eV, as in this paragraph.)

The charged W particles are responsible for processes, such as beta decay, in which the charge of the participating particles changes hands. For example, when a neutron transmutes into a proton, it emits a W^-. Thus, the overall charge remains zero before and after the decay process. The W particle involved in this process is a virtual particle. Because its mass is far greater than that of the neutron, the only way that it can be emitted by the lightweight neutron is for its existence to be fleetingly short, within the requirements of the uncertainty principle. Indeed, the W^- immediately transforms into an electron and an antineutrino, the particles that are observed in the laboratory as the products of neutron beta decay. Z particles are exchanged in similar reactions that involve no change in charge.

In the everyday world, the weak force is weaker than the electromagnetic force but stronger than the gravitational force. Its range, however, is particularly short. Because of the large amounts of energy needed to create

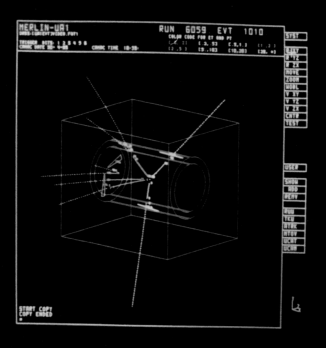

*Tracks emerging from a proton-antiproton collision at the centre of the UA1
detector at CERN include those of an energetic electron (straight down) and
a positron (upper right). These two particles have come from the decay of a
Z^0. When their energies are added together, the total is equal to the Z's mass.*
David Parker/Science Photo Library—Photo Researchers

the large masses of the W and Z particles, the uncertainty principle ensures that a weak gauge boson cannot be borrowed for long, which limits the range of the force to distances less than 10^{-17} metre, about 1 percent of the diameter of a typical atomic nucleus. The weak force between two protons in a nucleus is only 10^{-7} the strength of the electromagnetic force. In radioactive decays the strength of the weak force is about 100,000 times less than the strength of the electromagnetic force. As the electroweak theory reveals and as experiments confirm, however, this weak force becomes effectively stronger as the energies of the participating particles increase. When the energies reach 100 GeV or so—roughly the energy equivalent to the mass of the W and Z particles—the strength of the weak force becomes comparable to that of the electromagnetic force. This means that reactions that involve the exchange of a Z° become as common as those in which a photon is exchanged. Moreover, at these energies, real W and Z particles, as opposed to virtual ones, can be created in reactions.

Unlike the photon, which is stable and can in principle live forever, the heavy weak gauge bosons decay to lighter particles within an extremely brief lifetime of about 10^{-25} second. This is roughly a million million times shorter than experiments can measure directly, but physicists can detect the particles into which the W and Z particles decay and can thus infer their existence.

THE STRONG FORCE

Although the aptly named strong force is the strongest of all the fundamental interactions, it, like the weak force, is short-ranged and is ineffective much beyond nuclear distances of 10^{-15} metre or so. Within the nucleus and, more specifically, within the protons and other particles that are built from quarks, however, the strong force rules supreme. Between quarks in a proton, it can be almost 100 times stronger than the electromagnetic force, depending on the distance between the quarks.

During the 1970s physicists developed a theory for the strong force that is similar in structure to quantum electrodynamics. In this theory quarks are bound together within protons and neutrons by exchanging gauge bosons called gluons. The quarks carry a property called "colour" that is analogous to electric charge. Just as electrically charged particles experience the electromagnetic force and exchange photons, so colour-charged, or coloured, particles feel the strong force and exchange gluons. This property of colour gives rise in part to the name of the theory of the strong force: quantum chromodynamics.

Gluons are massless and have a spin quantum number of 1. In this respect they are much like photons, but they differ from photons in one crucial way. Whereas photons do not interact among themselves—because they are not electrically charged—gluons do carry colour charge. This means that gluons can interact together, which has an important effect in limiting the range of gluons and in confining quarks within protons and other particles.

There are three types of colour charge, called red, green, and blue, although there is no connection between the colour charge of quarks and gluons and colour in the usual sense. Quarks each carry a single colour charge, while gluons carry both a colour and an anticolour charge. Protons and neutrons are examples of baryons, a class of particles that contain three quarks, each with one of three possible values of colour (red, blue, and green).

The strong force acts in such a way that quarks of different colour are attracted to one another. Thus, red attracts green, blue attracts red, and so on. Quarks of the same colour, however, repel each other. The quarks can combine only in ways that give a net colour charge of zero. In particles that contain three quarks, such as protons, this is achieved by adding red, blue, and green.

An alternative, observed in particles called mesons, such as pi mesons and K mesons, is for a quark to couple with an antiquark of the same basic colour. In this case the colour of the quark and the anticolour of the antiquark cancel each other out. These combinations of three quarks (or three antiquarks) or of quark-antiquark pairs are the only combinations that the strong force seems to allow. Attempts to knock out individual quarks (in high-energy particle collisions, for example) result only in the creation of new "colourless" particles, mainly mesons.

The constraint that only colourless objects can appear in nature seems to limit attempts to observe single quarks and free gluons. Although a quark can radiate a real gluon just as an electron can radiate a real photon, the gluon never emerges on its own into the surrounding environment. Instead, it somehow creates additional gluons, quarks, and antiquarks from its own energy and materializes as normal particles built from quarks. Similarly, it appears that the strong force keeps quarks permanently confined within larger particles. Attempts to knock quarks out of protons by, for example, knocking protons together at high energies succeed only in creating more particles — that is, in releasing new quarks and antiquarks that are bound together and are themselves confined by the strong force.

FEYNMAN DIAGRAMS

Feynman diagrams are a graphical method of representing the interactions of elementary particles, invented in the 1940s and '50s by the American theoretical physicist Richard P. Feynman. Introduced during the development of the theory of quantum electrodynamics as an aid for visualizing and calculating the effects of

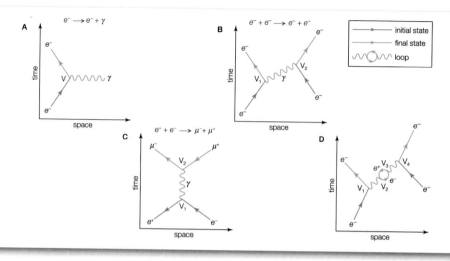

Feynman diagrams. (A) The interaction of an electron with the electromagnetic force. The basic vertex (V) shows the emission of a photon (γ) by an electron (e-). (B) The simplest interaction between two electrons. The two vertices (V1 and V2) represent the emission and absorption, respectively, of a photon (γ). (C) Annihilation of an electron by a positron (e+). The annihilation of the particle-antiparticle pair leads to the formation of a muon (μ-) and an antimuon (μ+). Both antiparticles (e+ and μ+) are represented as particles moving backward in time; that is, the arrowheads are reversed. (D) Feynman diagram of a complex interaction between two electrons, involving four vertices (V1, V2, V3, V4) and an electron-positron loop. Encyclopædia Britannica, Inc.

electromagnetic interactions among electrons and photons, Feynman diagrams are now used to depict all types of particle interactions.

A Feynman diagram is a two-dimensional representation in which one axis, usually the horizontal axis, is chosen to represent space, while the second (vertical) axis represents time. Straight lines are used to depict fermions—fundamental particles with half-integer values of intrinsic angular momentum (spin), such as electrons (e-)—and wavy lines are used for bosons—particles with integer values of spin, such as photons (γ). On a conceptual level fermions may be regarded as "matter" particles, which

Richard P. Feynman (shown here with his wife) illustrated particle interactions in what came to be known as Feynman diagrams. Keystone/Hulton Archive/Getty Images

experience the effect of a force arising from the exchange of bosons, so-called "force-carrier," or field, particles.

At the quantum level the interactions of fermions occur through the emission and absorption of the field particles associated with the fundamental interactions of matter, in particular the electromagnetic force, the strong force, and the weak force. The basic interaction therefore appears on a Feynman diagram as a "vertex" (i.e., a junction of three lines). In this way the path of an electron, for example, appears as two straight lines connected to a third, wavy, line where the electron emits or absorbs a photon.

Feynman diagrams are used by physicists to make very precise calculations of the probability of any given process, such as electron-electron scattering, for example, in quantum electrodynamics. The calculations must include terms equivalent to all the lines (representing propagating particles) and all the vertices (representing interactions) shown in the diagram. In addition, because a given process can be represented by many possible Feynman diagrams, the contributions of every possible diagram must be entered into the calculation of the total probability that a particular process will occur. Comparison of the results of these calculations with experimental measurements have revealed an extraordinary level of accuracy, with agreement to nine significant digits in some cases.

The simplest Feynman diagrams involve only two vertices, representing the emission and absorption of a field particle. For example, in such a diagram an electron (e^-) emits a photon at V_1, and this photon is then absorbed slightly later by another electron at V_2. The emission of the photon causes the first electron to recoil in space, while the absorption of the photon's energy and momentum causes a comparable deflection in the second electron's path. The result of this interaction is that the particles move away from each other in space.

One intriguing feature of Feynman diagrams is that antiparticles are represented as ordinary matter particles moving backward in time—that is, with the arrow head reversed on the lines that depict them. For example, in another typical interaction, an electron collides with its antiparticle, a positron (e^+), and both are annihilated. A photon is created by the collision, and it subsequently forms two new particles in space: a muon (μ^-) and its antiparticle, an antimuon (μ^+). In the diagram of this interaction, both antiparticles (e^+ and μ^+) are represented as their corresponding particles moving backward in time (toward the past). More complex Feynman diagrams, involving the emission and absorption of many particles, are also possible.

CLASSES OF SUBATOMIC PARTICLES

From the early 1930s to the mid-1960s, studies of the composition of cosmic rays and experiments using particle accelerators revealed more than 200 types of subatomic particles. In order to comprehend this rich variety, physicists began to classify the particles according to their properties (such as mass, charge, and spin) and to their behaviour in response to the fundamental interactions— in particular, the weak and strong forces. The aim was to discover common features that would simplify the variety, much as the periodic table of chemical elements had done for the wealth of atoms discovered in the 19th century. An important result was that many of the particles, those classified as hadrons, were found to be composed of a much smaller number of more-elementary particles, the quarks. Today the quarks, together with the group of leptons, are recognized as fundamental particles of matter.

Leptons and Antileptons

Leptons are a group of subatomic particles that do not experience the strong force. They do, however, feel the weak force and the gravitational force, and electrically charged leptons interact via the electromagnetic force.

CHARGED LEPTONS (ELECTRON, MUON, TAU)

In essence, there are three types of electrically charged leptons and three types of neutral leptons, together with six related antileptons. In all three cases the charged lepton has a negative charge, whereas its antiparticle is positively charged. Physicists coined the name *lepton* from the Greek word for "slender" because, before the discovery of the tau in 1975, it seemed that the leptons were the lightest particles. Although the name is no longer appropriate, it has been retained to describe all spin-½ particles that do not feel the strong force.

Electron

Probably the most-familiar subatomic particle is the electron, the component of atoms that makes interatomic bonding and chemical reactions—and hence life—possible. The electron was also the first particle to be discovered. Its negative charge of 1.6×10^{-19} coulomb seems to be the basic unit of electric charge, although theorists have a poor understanding of what determines this particular size.

The electron is the lightest stable subatomic particle known. The rest mass of the electron is 9.109×10^{-31} kg (or 0.511 megaelectron volts [MeV]; 10^6 eV), which is only $\frac{1}{1,840}$ the mass of a proton. An electron is therefore considered nearly massless in comparison with a proton or a neutron, and the electron mass is not included in calculating the mass number of an atom.

The electron was discovered in 1897 by the English physicist J.J. Thomson during investigations of cathode rays. His discovery of electrons, which he initially called corpuscles, played a pivotal role in revolutionizing knowledge of atomic structure. Under ordinary conditions electrons are bound to the positively charged nuclei of atoms by the attraction between opposite electric charges. In a neutral atom the number of electrons is identical to the number of positive charges on the nucleus. Any atom, however, may have more or fewer electrons than positive charges and thus be negatively or positively charged as a whole. These charged atoms are known as ions. Not all electrons are associated with atoms. Some occur in a free state with ions in the form of matter known as plasma.

Within any given atom, electrons move about the nucleus in an orderly arrangement of orbitals, the attraction between electrons and nucleus overcoming repulsion among the electrons that would otherwise cause them to fly apart. These orbitals are organized in concentric shells proceeding outward from the nucleus with an increasing number of subshells. The electrons in orbitals closest to the nucleus are held most tightly. Those in the outermost orbitals are shielded by intervening electrons and are the most loosely held by the nucleus. As the electrons move about within this structure, they form a diffuse cloud of negative charge that occupies nearly the entire volume of the atom. The detailed structural arrangement of electrons within an atom is referred to as the electronic configuration of the atom. The electronic configuration determines not only the size of an individual atom but also the chemical nature of the atom. The classification of elements within groups of similar elements in the periodic table, for example, is based on the similarity in their electron structures.

Muon

The next-heavier charged lepton is the muon. It has a mass of 106 MeV, which is 207 times greater than the electron's mass but is significantly less than the proton's mass of 938 MeV. Unlike the electron, which appears to be completely stable, the muon decays after an average lifetime of 2.2 millionths of a second into an electron, a neutrino, and an antineutrino. This process, like the beta decay of a neutron into a proton, an electron, and an antineutrino, occurs via the weak force. Experiments have shown that the intrinsic strength of the underlying reaction is the same in both kinds of decay, thus revealing that the weak force acts equally upon leptons (electrons, muons, neutrinos) and quarks (which form neutrons and protons). Because muons are charged, before decaying they lose energy by displacing electrons from atoms (ionization). At high velocities close to the speed of light, ionization dissipates energy in relatively small amounts, so muons in cosmic radiation are extremely penetrating and can travel thousands of metres below Earth's surface.

The muon was discovered as a constituent of cosmic-ray particle "showers" in 1936 by the American physicists Carl D. Anderson and Seth Neddermeyer. Because of its mass, it was at first thought to be the particle predicted by the Japanese physicist Yukawa Hideki in 1935 to explain the strong force that binds protons and neutrons together in atomic nuclei. It was subsequently discovered, however, that a muon is correctly assigned as a member of the lepton group of subatomic particles.

Tau

There is a third, heavier type of charged lepton, called the tau. The tau, with a mass of 1,777 MeV, is approximately 3,500 times heavier than the electron and is even heavier than the proton. Being so massive, the tau is unstable, with a mean life of 2.9×10^{-13} second, and it decays readily via the weak force into other particles. The tau can decay into a muon, plus a tau-neutrino and a muon-antineutrino. It can also decay directly into an electron, plus a tau-neutrino and an electron-antineutrino. Because the tau is heavy, it can also decay into particles containing quarks. In one example, the tau decays into particles called pi-mesons, which are accompanied by a tau-neutrino. The tau, like the electron and the muon, is associated with a corresponding neutral lepton, a tau-neutrino, that is produced in any decay reaction of a tau particle.

The tau was discovered through observations of its decay to muons and to electrons in the mid-1970s by a group led by Martin Perl at the Stanford Linear Accelerator Center in California. Perl named the new particle, the third charged lepton, after the Greek letter that begins the word *third*. In 2000 scientists at the Fermi National Accelerator Laboratory reported the first experimental evidence for the existence of the tau-neutrino, the tau's elusive partner.

NEUTRAL LEPTONS (NEUTRINO)

The neutral lepton, the neutrino, is an elementary subatomic particle with no electric charge, very little mass, and ½ unit of spin. There are three types of neutrino, each associated with a charged lepton (i.e., the electron, the muon, and the tau) and therefore given the corresponding names electron-neutrino, muon-neutrino, and tau-neutrino. Each type of neutrino also has an antimatter component, called an antineutrino. The term *neutrino* is sometimes used in a general sense to refer to both the neutrino and its antiparticle.

Although electrically neutral, the neutrinos seem to carry an identifying property that associates them specifically with one type of charged lepton. In the example of the muon's decay, the antineutrino produced is not simply the antiparticle of the neutrino that appears with it. The neutrino carries a muon-type hallmark, while the antineutrino, like the antineutrino emitted when a neutron decays, is always an electron-antineutrino. In interactions with matter, such electron-neutrinos and antineutrinos never produce muons, only electrons. Likewise, muon-neutrinos give rise to muons only, never to electrons.

The basic properties of the electron-neutrino—no electric charge and little mass—were predicted in 1930 by the Austrian physicist Wolfgang Pauli to explain the apparent loss of energy in the process of radioactive beta decay. The Italian-born physicist Enrico Fermi further elaborated (1934) the theory of beta decay and gave the "ghost" particle its name. An electron-neutrino is emitted along with a positron in positive beta decay, while an electron-antineutrino is emitted with an electron in negative beta decay.

Despite such predictions, neutrinos were not detected experimentally for 20 years, owing to the weakness of their interactions with matter. Because they are not electrically charged, unlike the charged leptons, neutrinos do not experience the electromagnetic force and thus do not cause ionization of matter. Furthermore, they react with matter only through the extremely weak interactions of gravity and the weak force. Neutrinos are therefore the most penetrating of subatomic particles, capable of passing through an enormous number of atoms without causing any reaction. Only 1 in 10 billion of these particles, traveling through matter for a distance equal to the Earth's diameter, reacts with a proton or a neutron. Finally, in 1956 a team of American physicists led by Frederick Reines reported the discovery of the electron-antineutrino. In their experiments antineutrinos emitted in a nuclear reactor were allowed to react with protons to produce neutrons and positrons. The unique (and rare) energy signatures of the fates of these latter by-products provided the evidence for the existence of the electron-antineutrino.

The discovery of the second type of charged lepton, the muon, became the starting point for the eventual identification of a second type of neutrino, the muon-neutrino. Identification of the muon-neutrino as distinct from the electron-neutrino was accomplished in 1962 on the basis of the results of a particle-accelerator experiment. High-energy muon-neutrinos were produced by decay of pi-mesons and were directed to a detector so that their reactions with matter could be studied. Although they are as unreactive as the other neutrinos, muon-neutrinos were found to produce muons but never electrons on the rare occasions when they reacted with protons or neutrons. The American physicists Leon Lederman, Melvin Schwartz, and Jack Steinberger received the 1988 Nobel Prize for Physics for having established the identity of muon-neutrinos. In 2000 physicists at the Fermi National Accelerator Laboratory reported the first experimental evidence for the existence of the tau-neutrino, which is associated with the third charged lepton, the tau.

All types of neutrino have masses much smaller than those of their charged partners. (Theory does not require the mass of neutrinos to be any specific amount, and in the past it was assumed to be zero.) For example, experiments show that the mass of the electron-neutrino must be less than 0.002 percent that of the electron and that the sum of the masses of the three types of neutrinos must be less than 0.48 electron volt. For many years it seemed that neutrinos' masses might be exactly zero, although there was no compelling theoretical reason why this should be so. Then in 2002 the Sudbury Neutrino Observatory (SNO), in Ontario, Canada, found the first direct evidence that electron-neutrinos emitted by nuclear reactions in the core of the Sun change type as they travel through the Sun. Such neutrino "oscillations" are possible only if one or more of the neutrino types has some small mass. Studies of neutrinos produced in the interactions of cosmic rays in Earth's atmosphere also indicate that neutrinos have mass, but further experiments are needed to understand the exact masses involved.

HADRONS

The name *hadron* comes from the Greek word for "strong." It refers to all those particles that are built from quarks and therefore experience the strong force. The most common examples of this class are the proton and the neutron, the two types of particle that build up the nucleus of every atom.

STABLE AND RESONANT HADRONS

Experiments have revealed a large number of hadrons, of which only the proton appears to be stable. Indeed, even if the proton is not absolutely stable, experiments show that its lifetime is at least in excess of 10^{32} years. In contrast, a single neutron, free from the forces at work within the nucleus, lives an average of nearly 15 minutes before decaying. Within a nucleus, however—even the simple nucleus of deuterium, which consists of one proton and one neutron—the balance of forces is sufficient to prolong the neutron's lifetime so that many nuclei are stable and a large variety of chemical elements exist.

Some hadrons typically exist only 10^{-10} to 10^{-8} second. Fortunately for experimentalists, these particles are usually born in such high-energy collisions that they are moving at velocities close to the speed of light. Their timescale is therefore "stretched" or "slowed down" so that, in the high-speed particle's frame of reference, its lifetime may be 10^{-10} second, but, in a stationary observer's frame of reference, the particle lives much longer.

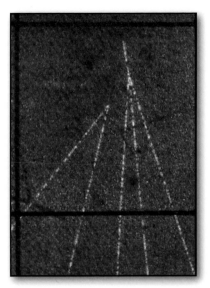

The "footprint" of a D^0 meson in a bubble chamber sensitive enough to reveal its brief life of 4×10^{-4} second. Because it is neutral, the D^0 leaves no track and is seen as a short gap before it decays into the two charged particles whose tracks form the inverted V on the left. By courtesy of the Stanford Linear Accelerator Center

This effect, known as time dilation in the theory of special relativity, allows stationary particle detectors to record the tracks left by these short-lived particles. These hadrons, which number about a dozen, are usually referred to as "stable" to distinguish them from still shorter-lived hadrons with lifetimes typically in the region of a mere 10^{-23} second.

The stable hadrons usually decay via the weak force. In some cases they decay by the electromagnetic force, which results in somewhat shorter lifetimes because the electromagnetic force is stronger than the weak force. The very-short-lived hadrons, however, which number 200 or more, decay via the strong force. This force is so strong that it allows the particles to live only for about the time it takes light to cross the particle. The particles decay almost as soon as they are created.

These very-short-lived particles are called "resonant" because they are observed as a resonance phenomenon. They are too short-lived to be observed in any other way. Resonance occurs when a system absorbs more energy than usual because the energy is being supplied at the system's own natural frequency. For example, soldiers break step when they cross a bridge because their rhythmic marching could make the bridge resonate—set it vibrating at its own natural frequency—so that it absorbs enough energy to cause damage. Subatomic-particle resonances occur when the net energy of colliding particles is just sufficient to create the rest mass of the new particle, which the strong force then breaks apart within 10^{-23} second. The absorption of energy, or its subsequent emission in the form of particles as the resonance decays, is revealed as the energy of the colliding particles is varied.

BARYONS AND MESONS

The hadrons, whether stable or resonant, fall into two classes: baryons and mesons. Originally the names referred to the relative masses of the two groups of particles. The baryons (from the Greek word for "heavy") included the proton and heavier particles. The mesons (from the Greek word for "between") were particles with masses between those of the electron and the proton. Now, however, the name *baryon* refers to any particle built from three quarks, such as the proton and the neutron. Mesons, on the other hand, are particles built from a quark combined with an antiquark. As described in the section The strong force, these are the only two combinations of quarks and antiquarks that the strong force apparently allows.

The two groups of hadrons are also distinguished from one another in terms of a property called baryon number. The baryons are characterized by a baryon number, B, of 1. Antibaryons have a baryon number of -1. The baryon number of the mesons, leptons, and messenger particles is 0. Baryon numbers are additive. Thus, an atom containing one proton and one neutron (each with a baryon number of 1) has a baryon number of 2. Quarks therefore must have a baryon number of $\frac{1}{3}$, and the antiquarks a baryon number of $-\frac{1}{3}$, in order to give the correct values of 1 or 0 when they combine to form baryons and mesons.

The empirical law of baryon conservation states that in any reaction the total number of baryons must remain constant. If any baryons are created, then so must be an equal number of antibaryons, which in principle negate the baryons. Conservation of baryon number explains the apparent stability of the proton. The proton does not decay into lighter positive particles, such as the positron or the mesons, because those particles have a baryon number of 0. Neutrons and other heavy baryons can decay into the lighter protons, however, because the total number of baryons present does not change.

At a more detailed level, baryons and mesons are differentiated from one another in terms of their spin. The basic quarks and antiquarks have a spin of ½ (which may be oriented in either of two directions). When three quarks combine to form a baryon, their spins can add up to only half-integer values. In contrast, when quarks and antiquarks combine to form mesons, their spins always add up to integer values. As a result, baryons are classified as fermions within the Standard Model of particle physics, whereas mesons are classified as bosons.

Predicted theoretically in 1935 by the Japanese physicist Yukawa Hideki, the existence of mesons was confirmed in 1947 by a team led by the English physicist Cecil Frank Powell with the discovery of the pi-meson (pion) in cosmic-ray particle interactions. More than 200 mesons have been produced and characterized in the intervening years, most in high-energy particle-accelerator experiments. All mesons are unstable, with lifetimes ranging from 10^{-8} second to less than 10^{-22} second. They also vary widely in mass, from 140 megaelectron volts (MeV; 10^6 eV) to nearly 10 gigaelectron volts (GeV; 10^9 eV). Mesons serve as a useful tool for studying the properties and interactions of quarks.

Despite their instability, many mesons last long enough (a few billionths of a second) to be observed with particle detectors, making it possible for researchers to reconstruct the motions of quarks. Any model attempting to explain quarks must correctly elucidate the behaviour of mesons. One of the early successes of the Eightfold Way—a forerunner of modern quark models devised by the physicists Murray Gell-Mann and Yuval Ne'eman—was the prediction and subsequent discovery of the eta-meson (1962). Some years later the decay rate of the pi-meson into two photons was used to support the hypothesis that quarks can take on one of three "colours."

Mesons also provide a means of identifying new quarks. The J/psi particle, discovered independently by teams led by the American physicists Samuel C.C. Ting and Burton Richter in 1974, proved to be a meson made up of a charm quark and its antiquark. (Up to this time, three quark types had been postulated—up, down, and strange.) It was the first manifestation of charm, a new quantum number the existence of which implies that quarks are related in pairs. The subsequent discovery of another heavy meson, called upsilon, revealed the existence of the bottom quark and its accompanying antiquark and gave rise to speculation about the existence of a companion particle, the top quark. This sixth quark type, or "flavour," was discovered in 1995. Conclusive proof of its existence culminated the search for one of the last missing pieces in the Standard Model of particle physics, which describes the fundamental particles and their interactions.

Proton

The proton is a stable subatomic particle that has a positive charge equal in magnitude to a unit of electron charge and a rest mass of 1.67262×10^{-27} kg, which is 1,836 times the mass of an electron.

Protons, together with electrically neutral particles called neutrons, make up all atomic nuclei except for the hydrogen nucleus (which consists of a single proton). Every nucleus of a given chemical element has the same number of protons. This number defines the atomic number of an element and determines the position of the element in the periodic table. When the number of protons in a nucleus equals the number of electrons orbiting the nucleus, the atom is electrically neutral.

The discovery of the proton dates to the earliest investigations of atomic structure. While studying streams of ionized gaseous atoms and molecules from which electrons had been stripped, Wilhelm Wien (1898) and J.J. Thomson (1910) identified a positive particle equal in mass to the hydrogen atom. Ernest Rutherford showed (1919) that nitrogen under alpha-particle bombardment ejects what appear to be hydrogen nuclei. By 1920 he had accepted the hydrogen nucleus as an elementary particle, naming it proton.

High-energy particle-physics studies in the late 20th century refined the structural understanding of the nature of the proton within the group of subatomic particles. Protons and neutrons have been shown to be made up of smaller particles and are classified as baryons.

Protons from ionized hydrogen are given high velocities in particle accelerators and are commonly used as projectiles to produce and study nuclear reactions. Protons are the chief constituent of primary cosmic rays and are among the products of some types of artificial nuclear reactions.

Neutron

The neutron is a neutral subatomic particle that is a constituent of every atomic nucleus except ordinary hydrogen. It has no electric charge and a rest mass equal to 1.67495×10^{-27} kg—marginally greater than that of the proton but nearly 1,840 times greater than that of the electron. Neutrons and protons, commonly called nucleons, are bound together in the dense inner core of an atom, the nucleus, where they account for 99.9 percent of the atom's mass. Developments in high-energy particle physics in the 20th century revealed that neither the neutron nor the proton is a true elementary particle. Rather, they are composites of extremely small elementary particles called quarks. The nucleus is bound together by the residual effect of the strong force, a fundamental interaction that governs the behaviour of the quarks that make up the individual protons and neutrons.

The neutron was discovered in 1932 by the English physicist James Chadwick. Within a few years after this discovery, many investigators throughout the world were studying the properties and interactions of the particle. It was found that various elements, when bombarded by neutrons, undergo fission—a type of nuclear reaction that occurs when the nucleus of a heavy element is split into two nearly equal smaller fragments. During this reaction each fissioned nucleus gives off additional free neutrons, as well as those bound to the fission fragments. In 1942 a group of American researchers, under the leadership of the physicist Enrico Fermi, demonstrated that enough free neutrons are produced during the fission process to sustain a chain reaction. This development led to the construction of the atomic bomb. Subsequent technological breakthroughs resulted in the large-scale production of electric power from nuclear energy. The absorption of neutrons by nuclei exposed to the high neutron intensities available in nuclear reactors has also made it possible to produce large quantities of radioactive isotopes useful for a wide variety of purposes. Furthermore, the neutron has become an important tool in pure research. Knowledge of its properties and structure is essential to an understanding of the structure of matter in general. Nuclear reactions induced by neutrons are valuable sources of information about the atomic nucleus and the force that binds it together.

A free neutron—one that is not incorporated into a nucleus—is subject to radioactive decay of a type called beta decay. It breaks down into a proton, an electron, and an antineutrino (the antimatter counterpart of the neutrino, a particle with no charge and little or no mass). The half-life for this decay process is 614 seconds. Because it readily disintegrates in this manner, the neutron does not exist in nature in its free state, except among other highly energetic particles in cosmic rays. Since free neutrons are electrically neutral, they pass unhindered through the electrical fields within atoms and so constitute a penetrating form of radiation, interacting with matter almost exclusively through relatively rare collisions with atomic nuclei.

QUARKS AND ANTIQUARKS

The baryons and mesons are complex subatomic particles built from more elementary objects, the quarks. Throughout the 1960s theoretical physicists, trying to account for the ever-growing number of subatomic particles observed in experiments, considered the possibility that protons and neutrons were composed of smaller units of matter. In 1961 two physicists, Murray Gell-Mann of the United States and Yuval Ne'eman of Israel, proposed a particle classification scheme called the Eightfold Way, based on the mathematical symmetry group SU(3), which described strongly interacting particles in terms of building blocks. In 1964 Gell-Mann introduced the concept of quarks as a physical basis for the scheme, having adopted the fanciful term from a passage in James Joyce's novel *Finnegans Wake*. (The American physicist George Zweig developed a similar theory independently that same year and called his fundamental particles "aces.") Gell-Mann's model provided a simple picture in which all mesons are shown as consisting of a quark and an antiquark and all baryons as composed of three quarks. It postulated the existence of three types of quarks, distinguished by unique "flavours." These three quark types are now commonly designated as "up" (u), "down" (d), and "strange" (s). Each carries a fractional value of the electron charge (i.e., a charge less than that of the electron, e). The up quark (charge $\frac{2}{3}e$) and down quark (charge $-\frac{1}{3}e$) make up protons and neutrons and are thus the ones observed in ordinary matter. Strange quarks (charge $-\frac{1}{3}e$) occur as components of K mesons and various other extremely short-lived subatomic particles that were first observed in cosmic rays but that play no part in ordinary matter.

Six types of quarks, together with their corresponding antiquarks, are necessary to account for all the known hadrons. The six varieties, or "flavours," of quark have acquired the names up, down, charm, strange, top, and bottom. The meaning of these somewhat unusual names is not important. They have arisen for a number of reasons. What is important is the way that the quarks contribute to matter at different levels and the properties that they bear.

The quarks are unusual in that they carry electric charges that are smaller in magnitude than e, the size of the charge of the electron (1.6×10^{-19} coulomb). This is necessary if quarks are to combine together to give the correct electric charges for the observed particles, usually 0, $+e$, or $-e$. Only two types of quark are necessary to build protons and neutrons, the constituents of atomic nuclei. These are the up quark, with a charge of $+ \frac{2}{3}e$, and the down quark, which has a charge of $- \frac{1}{3}e$. The proton consists of two up quarks and one down quark, which gives it a total charge of $+e$. The neutron, however, is built from one up quark and two down quarks, so that it has a net charge of zero. The other properties of the up and down quarks also add together to give the measured values for the proton and neutron. For example, the quarks have spins of ½. In order to form a proton or a neutron, which also have spin ½, the quarks must align in such a way that two of the three spins cancel each other, leaving a net value of ½.

Up and down quarks can also combine to form particles other than protons and neutrons. For example, the spins of the three quarks can be arranged so that they do not cancel. In this case they form short-lived resonance states, which have been given the name delta, or Δ. The deltas have spins of $\frac{3}{2}$, and the up and down quarks combine in four possible configurations—*uuu, uud, udd,* and *ddd*—where *u* and *d* stand for up and down. The charges of these Δ states are $+2e$, $+e$, 0, and $-e$, respectively.

The up and down quarks can also combine with their antiquarks to form mesons. The pi-meson, or pion, which is the lightest meson and an important component of cosmic rays, exists in three forms: with charge e (or 1), with charge 0, and with charge $-e$ (or -1). In the positive state an up quark combines with a down antiquark. A down quark together with an up antiquark compose the negative pion. The neutral pion is a quantum mechanical mixture of two states—$u\bar{u}$ and $d\bar{d}$, where the bar over the top of the letter indicates the antiquark.

Up and down are the lightest varieties of quarks. Somewhat heavier are a second pair of quarks, charm (c) and strange (s), with charges of $+\frac{2}{3}e$ and $-\frac{1}{3}e$, respectively. A third, still heavier pair of quarks consists of top (or truth, t) and bottom (or beauty, b), again with charges of $+\frac{2}{3}e$ and $-\frac{1}{3}e$, respectively. These heavier quarks and their antiquarks combine with up and down quarks and with each other to produce a range of hadrons, each of which is heavier than the basic proton and pion, which represent the lightest varieties of baryon and meson, respectively. For example, the particle called lambda (Λ) is a baryon built from u, d, and s quarks. Thus, it is like the neutron but with a d quark replaced by an s quark.

The interpretation of quarks as actual physical entities initially posed two major problems. First, quarks had to have half-integer spin (intrinsic angular momentum) values for the model to work, but at the same time they seemed to violate the Pauli exclusion principle, which governs the behaviour of all particles (called fermions) having odd half-integer spin. In many of the baryon configurations constructed of quarks, sometimes two or even three identical quarks had to be set in the same quantum state—an arrangement prohibited by the exclusion principle. Second, quarks appeared to defy being freed from the particles they made up. Although the forces binding quarks were strong, it seemed improbable that they were powerful enough to withstand bombardment by high-energy particle beams from accelerators.

These problems were resolved by the introduction of the concept of colour, as formulated in quantum chromodynamics (QCD, which is described in further detail below). In this theory of strong interactions, whose breakthrough ideas were published in 1973, colour has nothing to do with the colours of the everyday world but rather represents a property of quarks that is the source of the strong force. The colours red, green, and blue are ascribed to quarks, and their opposites, antired, antigreen, and antiblue, are ascribed to antiquarks. According to QCD, all combinations of quarks must contain mixtures of these imaginary colours that cancel out one another, with the resulting particle having no net colour. A baryon, for example, always consists of a combination of one red, one green, and one blue quark and so never violates the exclusion principle. The property of colour in the strong force plays a role analogous to that of electric charge in the electromagnetic force, and just as charge implies the exchange of photons between charged particles, so does colour involve the exchange of massless particles called gluons among quarks. Just as photons carry electromagnetic force, gluons transmit the forces that bind quarks together. Quarks change their colour as they emit and absorb gluons, and the exchange of gluons maintains proper quark colour distribution.

The binding forces carried by the gluons tend to be weak when quarks are close together. Within a proton (or other hadron), at distances of less than 10^{-15} metre, quarks behave as though they were nearly free. This condition is called asymptotic freedom. When one begins to draw the quarks apart, however, as when attempting to knock them out of a proton, the effect of the force grows stronger.

This is because, as explained by QCD, gluons have the ability to create other gluons as they move between quarks. Thus, if a quark starts to speed away from its companions after being struck by an accelerated particle, the gluons use energy that they draw from the quark's motion to produce more gluons. The larger the number of gluons exchanged among quarks, the stronger the effective binding forces become. Supplying additional energy to extract the quark only results in the conversion of that energy into new quarks and antiquarks with which the first quark combines. This phenomenon is observed at high-energy particle accelerators in the production of "jets" of new particles that can be associated with a single quark.

The discovery in the 1970s of the "charm" (c) and "bottom" (b) quarks and their associated antiquarks, achieved through the creation of mesons, strongly suggests that quarks occur in pairs. This speculation led to efforts to find a sixth type of quark called "top" (t), after its proposed flavour. According to theory, the top quark carries a charge of $\frac{2}{3}e$. Its partner, the bottom quark, has a charge of $-\frac{1}{3}e$. In 1995 two independent groups of scientists at the Fermi National Accelerator Laboratory reported that they had found the top quark. The top quark has a mass of 171.3 & 2.3 gigaelectron volts (GeV; 10^9 eV). (The next heaviest quark, the bottom, has a mass of 4.2 GeV.) It has yet to be explained why the top quark is so much more massive than the other elementary particles, but its existence completes the Standard Model, the prevailing theoretical scheme of nature's fundamental building blocks.

CHAPTER 2
THE DEVELOPMENT OF
MODERN PARTICLE THEORY

The year of the birth of particle physics is often cited as 1932. Near the beginning of that year James Chadwick, working in England at the Cavendish Laboratory in Cambridge, discovered the existence of the neutron. This discovery seemed to complete the picture of atomic structure that had begun with Ernest Rutherford's work at the University of Manchester, England, in 1911, when it became apparent that almost all of the mass of an atom was concentrated in a nucleus. The elementary particles seemed firmly established as the proton, the neutron, and the electron. By the end of 1932, however, Carl Anderson in the United States had discovered the first antiparticle— the positron, or antielectron. Moreover, Patrick Blackett and Giuseppi Occhialini, working, like Chadwick, at the Cavendish Laboratory, had revealed how positrons and electrons are created in pairs when cosmic rays pass through dense matter. It was becoming apparent that the simple pictures provided by electrons, protons, and neutrons were incomplete and that a new theory was needed to explain fully the phenomena of subatomic particles.

QUANTUM ELECTRODYNAMICS: DESCRIBING THE ELECTROMAGNETIC FORCE

The English physicist P.A.M. Dirac had provided the foundations for such a theory in 1927 with his quantum theory of the electromagnetic field. Dirac's theory treated the electromagnetic field as a "gas" of photons (the quanta

English physicist P.A.M. Dirac is renowned for his relativistic quantum theory of the electron as well as his calculation of the existence of antiparticles.
Boyer/Roger Viollet/Getty Images

of light), and it yielded a correct description of the absorption and emission of radiation by electrons in atoms. It was the first quantum field theory.

A year later Dirac published his relativistic electron theory, which took correct account of Albert Einstein's theory of special relativity. Dirac's theory showed that the electron must have a spin quantum number of ½ and a magnetic moment. It also predicted the existence of the positron, although Dirac did not at first realize this and puzzled over what seemed like extra solutions to his equations. Only with Anderson's discovery of the positron did the picture become clear: radiation, a photon, can produce electrons and positrons in pairs, provided the energy of the photon is greater than the total mass-energy of the two particles — that is, about 1 megaelectron volt (MeV; 10^6 eV).

Dirac's quantum field theory was a beginning, but it explained only one aspect of the electromagnetic interactions between radiation and matter. During the following years other theorists began to extend Dirac's ideas to form a comprehensive theory of quantum electrodynamics (QED) that would account fully for the interactions of charged particles not only with radiation but also with one another. One important step was to describe the electrons in terms of fields, in analogy to the electromagnetic field of the photons. This enabled theorists to describe everything in terms of quantum field theory. It also helped to cast light on Dirac's positrons.

According to QED, a vacuum is filled with electron-positron fields. Real electron-positron pairs are created when energetic photons, represented by the electromagnetic field, interact with these fields. Virtual electron-positron pairs, however, can also exist for minute durations, as dictated by Heisenberg's uncertainty principle, and this at first led to fundamental difficulties with QED.

During the 1930s it became clear that, as it stood, QED gave the wrong answers for quite simple problems. For example, the theory said that the emission and reabsorption of the same photon would occur with an infinite probability. This led in turn to infinities occurring in many situations. Even the mass of a single electron was infinite according to QED because, on the timescales of the uncertainty principle, the electron could continuously emit and absorb virtual photons.

It was not until the late 1940s that a number of theorists working independently resolved the problems with QED. Julian Schwinger and Richard Feynman in the United States and Tomonaga Shin'ichirō in Japan proved that they could rid the theory of its embarrassing infinities by a process known as renormalization. Basically, renormalization acknowledges all possible infinities and then allows the positive infinities to cancel the negative ones. The mass and charge of the electron, which are infinite in theory, are then defined to be their measured values.

Once these steps have been taken, QED works beautifully. It is the most accurate quantum field theory scientists have at their disposal. In recognition of their achievement, Feynman, Schwinger, and Tomonaga were awarded the Nobel Prize for Physics in 1965. Dirac had been similarly honoured in 1933.

QUANTUM CHROMODYNAMICS: DESCRIBING THE STRONG FORCE

As early as 1920, when Ernest Rutherford named the proton and accepted it as a fundamental particle, it was clear that the electromagnetic force was not the only force at work within the atom. Something stronger had to be responsible for binding the positively charged protons together and thereby overcoming their natural electrical repulsion. The discovery in 1932 of the neutron showed that there are (at least) two kinds of particles subject to the same force. Later in the same year, Werner Heisenberg in Germany made one of the first attempts to develop a quantum field theory that was analogous to QED but appropriate to the nuclear binding force.

THE NUCLEAR BINDING FORCE

According to quantum field theory, particles can be held together by a "charge-exchange" force, which is carried by charged intermediary particles. Heisenberg's application of this theory gave birth to the idea that the proton and neutron were charged and neutral versions of the same particle—an idea that seemed to be supported by the fact that the two particles have almost equal masses. Heisenberg proposed that a proton, for example, could emit a positively charged particle that was then absorbed by a neutron. The proton thus became a neutron, and vice versa. The nucleus was no longer viewed as a collection of two kinds of immutable billiard balls but rather as a continuously changing collection of protons and neutrons that were bound together by the exchange particles flitting between them.

Heisenberg believed that the exchange particle involved was an electron (he did not have many particles from which to choose). This electron had to have some rather odd characteristics, however, such as no spin and no magnetic moment, and this made Heisenberg's theory ultimately unacceptable. Quantum field theory did not seem applicable to the nuclear binding force. Then in 1935 a Japanese theorist, Yukawa Hideki, took a bold step: he invented a new particle as the carrier of the nuclear binding force.

The size of a nucleus shows that the binding force must be short-ranged, confining protons and neutrons within distances of about 10^{-14} metre. Yukawa argued that, to give this limited range, the force must involve the exchange of particles with mass, unlike the massless photons of QED. According to the uncertainty principle, exchanging a particle with mass sets a limit on the time allowed for the exchange and therefore restricts the range of the resulting force. Yukawa calculated a mass of about 200 times the electron's mass, or 100 MeV, for the new intermediary. Because the predicted mass of the new particle was between those of the electron and the proton, the particle was named the mesotron, later shortened to meson.

Yukawa's work was little known outside Japan until 1937, when Carl Anderson and his colleague Seth Neddermeyer announced that, five years after Anderson's discovery of the positron, they had found a second new particle in cosmic radiation. The new particle seemed to have exactly the mass Yukawa had prescribed and thus was seen as confirmation of Yukawa's theory by the Americans J. Robert Oppenheimer and Robert Serber, who made Yukawa's work more widely known in the West.

In the following years, however, it became clear that there were difficulties in reconciling the properties expected for Yukawa's intermediary particle with those of the new cosmic-ray particle. In particular, as a group of Italian physicists succeeded in demonstrating (while hiding from the occupying German forces during World War II), the cosmic-ray particles penetrate matter far too easily to be related to the nuclear binding force. To resolve this apparent paradox, theorists both in Japan and in the United States had begun to think that there might be two mesons. The two-meson theory proposed that Yukawa's nuclear meson decays into the penetrating meson observed in the cosmic rays.

In 1947 scientists at Bristol University in England found the first experimental evidence of two mesons in cosmic rays high on the Pic du Midi in France. Using detectors equipped with special photographic emulsion that can record the tracks of charged particles, the physicists at Bristol found the decay of a heavier meson into a lighter one. They called the heavier particle π (or pi), and it has since become known as the pi-meson, or pion. The lighter particle was dubbed μ (or mu) and is now known simply as the muon. (According to the modern definition of a meson as a particle consisting of a quark bound with an antiquark, the muon is not actually a meson. It is classified as a lepton—a relation of the electron.)

Studies of pions produced in cosmic radiation and in the first particle accelerators showed that the pion behaves precisely as expected for Yukawa's particle. Moreover, experiments confirmed that positive, negative, and neutral varieties of pions exist, as predicted by Nicholas Kemmer in England in 1938. Kemmer regarded the nuclear binding force as symmetrical with respect to the charge of the particles involved. He proposed that the nuclear force between protons and protons or between neutrons and neutrons is the same as the one between protons and neutrons. This symmetry required the existence of a neutral intermediary that did not figure in Yukawa's original theory. It also established the concept of a new "internal" property of subatomic particles—isospin.

Kemmer's work followed to some extent the trail Heisenberg had begun in 1932. Close similarities between nuclei containing the same total number of protons and neutrons, but in different combinations, suggest that protons can be exchanged for neutrons and vice versa without altering the net effect of the nuclear binding force. In other words, the force recognizes no difference between protons and neutrons. It is symmetrical under the interchange of protons and neutrons, rather as a square is symmetrical under rotations through 90°, 180°, and so on.

To introduce this symmetry into the theory of the nuclear force, it proved useful to adopt the mathematics describing the spin of particles. In this respect the proton and neutron are seen as different states of a single basic nucleon. These states are differentiated by an internal property that can have two values, + ½ and - ½, in analogy with the spin of a particle such as the electron. This new property is called isotopic spin, or isospin for short, and the nuclear binding force is said to exhibit isospin symmetry.

Symmetries are important in physics because they simplify the theories needed to describe a range of observations. For example, as far as physicists can tell, all physical laws exhibit translational symmetry. This means that the results of an experiment performed at one location in space and time can be used to predict correctly the outcome of the same experiment in another part of space and time. This symmetry is reflected in the conservation of momentum — the fact that the total momentum of a system remains constant unless it is acted upon by an external force.

Isospin symmetry is an important symmetry in particle physics, although it occurs only in the action of the nuclear binding force — or, in modern terminology, the strong force. The symmetry leads to the conservation of isospin in nuclear interactions that occur via the strong force and thereby determines which reactions can occur.

"STRANGENESS"

The discovery of the pion in 1947 seemed to restore order to the study of particle physics, but this order did not last long. Later in the year Clifford Butler and George Rochester, two British physicists studying cosmic rays, discovered the first examples of yet another type of new particle. The new particles were heavier than the pion or muon but lighter than the proton, with a mass of about 800 times the electron's mass. Within the next few years, researchers found copious examples of these particles, as well as other new particles that were heavier even than the proton. The evidence seemed to indicate that these particles were created in strong interactions in nuclear matter, yet the particles lived for a relatively long time without themselves interacting strongly with matter. This strange behaviour in some ways echoed the earlier problem with Yukawa's supposed meson, but the solution for the new "strange" particles proved to be different.

By 1953 at least four different kinds of strange particles had been observed. In an attempt to bring order into this increasing number of subatomic particles, Murray Gell-Mann in the United States and Nishijima Kazuhiko in Japan independently suggested a new conservation law. They argued that the strange particles must possess some new property, dubbed "strangeness," that is conserved in the strong nuclear reactions in which the particles are created. In the decay of the particles, however, a different, weaker force is at work, and this weak force does not conserve strangeness—as with isospin symmetry, which is respected only by the strong force.

According to this proposal, particles are assigned a strangeness quantum number, S, which can have only integer values. The pion, proton, and neutron have $S = 0$. Because the strong force conserves strangeness, it can produce strange particles only in pairs, in which the net value of strangeness is zero. This phenomenon, the importance of which was recognized by both Nishijima and the American physicist Abraham Pais in 1952, is known as associated production.

SU(3) SYMMETRY

With the introduction of strangeness, physicists had several properties with which they could label the various subatomic particles. In particular, values of mass, electric charge, spin, isospin, and strangeness gave physicists a means of classifying the strongly interacting particles—or

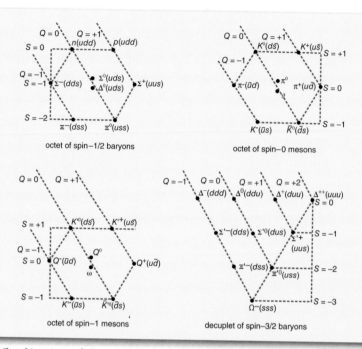

Combinations of the quarks u, d, and s and their corresponding antiquarks to form hadrons. The octets (hexagons) and the decuplet arise when particles are grouped according to strangeness, S, and charge, Q. Copyright Encyclopædia Britannica; rendering for this edition by Rosen Educational Services

hadrons—and of establishing a hierarchy of relationships between them. In 1962 Gell-Mann and Yuval Ne'eman, an Israeli scientist, independently showed that a particular type of mathematical symmetry provides the kind of grouping of hadrons that is observed in nature. The name of the mathematical symmetry is SU(3), which stands for "special unitary group in three dimensions."

SU(3) contains subgroups of objects that are related to each other by symmetrical transformations, rather as a group describing the rotations of a square through 90° contains the four symmetrical positions of the square. Gell-Mann and Ne'eman both realized that the basic subgroups of SU(3) contain either 8 or 10 members and that the observed hadrons can be grouped together in 8s or 10s in the same way. (The classification of the hadron class of subatomic particles into groups on the basis of their symmetry properties is also referred to as the Eightfold Way.) For example, the proton, neutron, and their relations with spin ½ fall into one octet, or group of 8, while the pion and its relations with spin 0 fit into another octet. A group of 9 very short-lived resonance particles with spin ³⁄₂ could be seen to fit into a decuplet, or group of 10, although at the time the classification was introduced, the 10th member of the group, the particle known as the Ω^- (or omega-minus), had not yet been observed. Its discovery early in 1964, at the Brookhaven National Laboratory in Upton, N.Y., confirmed the validity of the SU(3) symmetry of the hadrons.

THE DEVELOPMENT OF QUARK THEORY

The beauty of the SU(3) symmetry does not, however, explain why it holds true. Gell-Mann and another American physicist, George Zweig, independently decided in 1964 that the answer to that question lies in the fundamental nature of the hadrons. The most basic subgroup of SU(3) contains only three objects, from which the octets and decuplets can be built. The two theorists made the bold suggestion that the hadrons observed at the time were not simple structures but were instead built from three basic particles. Gell-Mann called these particles quarks—the name that remains in use today.

By the time Gell-Mann and Zweig put forward their ideas, the list of known subatomic particles had grown from the three of 1932—electron, proton, and neutron—to include most of the stable hadrons and a growing number of short-lived resonances, as well as the muon and two types of neutrino. That the seemingly ever-increasing number of hadrons could be understood in terms of only three basic building blocks was remarkable indeed. For this to be possible, however, those building blocks—the quarks—had to have some unusual properties.

These properties were so odd that for a number of years it was not clear whether quarks actually existed or were simply a useful mathematical fiction. For example, quarks must have charges of $+ \frac{2}{3}e$ or $- \frac{1}{3}e$, which should be very easy to spot in certain kinds of detectors. But intensive searches, both in cosmic rays and using particle accelerators, have never revealed any convincing evidence for fractional charge of this kind. By the mid-1970s, however, 10 years after quarks were first proposed, scientists had compiled a mass of evidence that showed that quarks do exist but are locked within the individual hadrons in such a way that they can never escape as single entities.

This evidence resulted from experiments in which beams of electrons, muons, or neutrinos were fired at the protons and neutrons in such target materials as hydrogen (protons only), deuterium, carbon, and aluminum. The incident particles used were all leptons, particles that do not feel the strong binding force and that were known, even then, to be much smaller than the nuclei they were probing. The scattering of the beam particles caused by interactions within the target clearly demonstrated that protons and neutrons are complex structures that contain structureless, pointlike objects, which were named partons because they are parts of the larger particles. The experiments also showed that the partons can indeed have fractional charges of $+ \frac{2}{3}e$ or $- \frac{1}{3}e$ and thus confirmed one of the more surprising predictions of the quark model.

Gell-Mann and Zweig required only three quarks to build the particles known in 1964. These quarks are the ones known as up (u), down (d), and strange (s). Since then, experiments have revealed a number of heavy hadrons—both mesons and baryons—which show that there are more than three quarks. Indeed, the SU(3) symmetry is part of a larger mathematical symmetry that incorporates quarks of several "flavours"—the term used to distinguish the different quarks. In addition to the up, down, and strange quarks, there are quarks known as charm (c), bottom (or beauty, b), and top (or truth, t). These quark flavours are all conserved during reactions that occur through the strong force. In other words, charm must be created in association with anticharm, bottom with antibottom, and so on. This implies that the quarks can change from one flavour to another only by way of the weak force, which is responsible for the decay of particles.

The up and down quarks are distinguished mainly by their differing electric charges, while the heavier quarks each carry a unique quantum number related to their flavour. The strange quark has strangeness, $S = -1$, the charm quark has charm, $C = +1$, and so on. Thus, three strange quarks together give a particle with an electric charge of $-e$ and a strangeness of -3, just as is required for the omega-minus (Ω^-) particle. The neutral strange particle known as the lambda (Λ) particle contains uds, which gives the correct total charge of o and a strangeness of -1. Using this system, the lambda can be viewed as a neutron with one down quark changed to a strange quark. Charge and spin remain the same, but the strange quark makes the lambda heavier than the neutron. Thus, the quark model reveals that nature is not arbitrary when it produces particles but is in some sense repeating itself on a more massive scale.

COLOUR

The realization in the late 1960s that protons, neutrons, and even Yukawa's pions are all built from quarks changed the direction of thinking about the nuclear binding force. Although at the level of nuclei Yukawa's picture remained valid, at the more minute quark level it could not satisfactorily explain what held the quarks together within the protons and pions or what prevented the quarks from escaping one at a time.

The answer to questions like these seems to lie in the property called colour. Colour was originally introduced to solve a problem raised by the exclusion principle that was formulated by the Austrian physicist Wolfgang Pauli in 1925. This rule does not allow particles with spin ½, such as quarks, to occupy the same quantum state. However, the omega-minus particle, for example, contains three quarks of the same flavour, sss, and has spin $\frac{3}{2}$, so the quarks must also all be in the same spin state. The omega-minus particle, according to the Pauli exclusion principle, should not exist.

To resolve this paradox, in 1964–65 Oscar Greenberg in the United States and Yoichiro Nambu and colleagues in Japan proposed the existence of a new property with three possible states. In analogy to the three primary colours of light, the new property became known as colour and the three varieties as red, green, and blue.

The three colour states and the three anticolour states (ascribed to antiquarks) are comparable to the two states of electric charge and anticharge (positive and negative), and hadrons are analogous to atoms. Just as atoms contain constituents whose electric charges balance overall to give a neutral atom, hadrons consist of coloured quarks that balance to give a particle with no net colour. Moreover, nuclei can be built from colourless protons and neutrons, rather as molecules form from electrically neutral atoms. Even Yukawa's pion exchange can be compared to exchange models of chemical bonding.

This analogy between electric charge and colour led to the idea that colour could be the source of the force between quarks, just as electric charge is the source of the electromagnetic force between charged particles. The colour force was seen to be working not between nucleons, as in Yukawa's theory, but between quarks. In the late 1960s and early 1970s, theorists turned their attention to developing a quantum field theory based on coloured quarks. In such a theory colour would take the role of electric charge in QED.

It was obvious that the field theory for coloured quarks had to be fundamentally different from QED because there are three kinds of colour as opposed to two states of electric charge. To give neutral objects, electric charges combine with an equal number of anticharges, as in atoms where the number of negative electrons equals the number of positive protons. With colour, however, three different charges must add together to give zero. In addition, because SU(3) symmetry (the same type of mathematical symmetry that Gell-Mann and Ne'eman used for three flavours) applies to the three colours, quarks of one colour must be able to transform into another colour. This implies that a quark can emit something—the quantum of the field due to colour—that itself carries colour. And if the field quanta are coloured, then they can interact between themselves, unlike the photons of QED, which are electrically neutral.

Despite these differences, the basic framework for a field theory based on colour already existed by the late 1960s, owing in large part to the work of theorists, particularly Chen Ning Yang and Robert Mills in the United States, who had studied similar theories in the 1950s. The new theory of the strong force was called quantum chromodynamics, or QCD, in analogy to quantum electrodynamics, or QED. In QCD the source of the field is the property of colour, and the field quanta are called gluons. Eight gluons are necessary in all to make the changes between the coloured quarks according to the rules of SU(3).

Asymptotic Freedom

In the early 1970s the American physicists David J. Gross and Frank Wilczek (working together) and H. David Politzer (working independently) discovered that the strong force between quarks becomes weaker at smaller distances and that it becomes stronger as the quarks move apart, thus preventing the separation of an individual quark. This is completely unlike the behaviour of the electromagnetic force. The quarks have been compared to prisoners on a chain gang. When they are close together, they can move freely and do not notice the chains binding them. If one quark/prisoner tries to move away, however, the strength of the chains is felt, and escape is prevented. This behaviour has been attributed to the fact that the virtual gluons that flit between the quarks within a hadron are not neutral but carry mixtures of colour and anticolour. The farther away a quark moves, the more gluons appear, each contributing to the net force. When the quarks are close together, they exchange fewer gluons, and the force is weaker. Only at infinitely close distances are quarks free, an effect known as asymptotic freedom. For their discovery of this effect, Gross, Wilczek, and Politzer were awarded the 2004 Nobel Prize for Physics.

The strong coupling between the quarks and gluons makes QCD a difficult theory to study. Mathematical procedures that work in QED cannot be used in QCD. The theory has nevertheless had a number of successes in describing the observed behaviour of particles in

H. David Politzer (left) worked with partners David J. Gross and Frank Wilczek to discover the effect known as asymptomatic freedom, for which the three were awarded the 2004 Nobel Prize for Physics. Henrik Montgomery/ AFP/Getty Images

experiments, and theorists are confident that it is the correct theory to use for describing the strong force.

ELECTROWEAK THEORY: DESCRIBING THE WEAK FORCE

The strong force binds particles together. By binding quarks within protons and neutrons, it indirectly binds protons and neutrons together to form nuclei. Nuclei can, however, break apart, or decay, naturally in the process known as radioactivity.

The electroweak theory describes both the electromagnetic force and the weak force. Superficially, these forces appear quite different. The weak force acts only across distances smaller than the atomic nucleus, while the electromagnetic force can extend for great distances (as observed in the light of stars reaching across entire galaxies), weakening only with the square of the distance. Moreover, comparison of the strength of these two fundamental interactions between two protons, for instance, reveals that the weak force is some 10 million times weaker than the electromagnetic force. Yet one of the major discoveries of the 20th century has been that these two forces are different facets of a single, more fundamental electroweak force.

The electroweak theory arose principally out of attempts to produce a self-consistent gauge theory for the weak force, in analogy with quantum electrodynamics (QED), the successful modern theory of the electromagnetic force developed during the 1940s. There are two basic requirements for the gauge theory of the weak force. First, it should exhibit an underlying mathematical symmetry, called gauge invariance, such that the effects of the force are the same at different points in space and time. Second, the theory should be renormalizable. That is, it should not contain nonphysical infinite quantities. In the following section, the history of the electroweak theory is discussed in greater detail.

BETA DECAY

One type of radioactivity, called beta decay, in which a nucleus emits an electron and thereby increases its net positive charge by one unit, has been known since the late 1890s. It was only with the discovery of the neutron in 1932 that physicists could begin to understand correctly what happens in this radioactive process.

The most basic form of beta decay involves the transmutation of a neutron into a proton, accompanied by the emission of an electron to keep the balance of electric charge. In addition, as Wolfgang Pauli realized in 1930, the neutron emits a neutral particle that shares the energy released by the decay. This neutral particle has little or no mass and is now known to be an antineutrino, the antiparticle of the neutrino. On its own, a neutron will decay in this way after an average lifetime of 15 minutes. Only within the confines of certain nuclei does the balance of forces prevent neutrons from decaying and thereby keep the entire nucleus stable.

A UNIVERSAL WEAK FORCE

The rates of nuclear decay indicate that any force involved in beta decay must be much weaker than the force that binds nuclei together. It may seem counterintuitive to think of a nuclear force that can disrupt the nucleus. However, the transformation of a neutron into a proton that occurs in neutron decay is comparable to the transformations by exchange of pions that Yukawa suggested to explain the nuclear binding force. Indeed, Yukawa's theory originally tried to explain both kinds of phenomena—weak decay and strong binding—with the exchange of a single type of particle. To give the different strengths, he proposed that the exchange particle couples strongly to the heavy neutrons and protons and weakly to the light electrons and neutrinos.

Yukawa was foreshadowing future developments in unifying the two nuclear forces in this way. However, as is explained in the following text, he had chosen the wrong two forces. He was also bold in incorporating two "new" particles in his theory—the necessary exchange particle and the neutrino predicted by Pauli only five years previously.

Pauli had been hesitant in suggesting that a second particle must be emitted in beta decay, even though that would explain why the electron could leave with a range of energies. Such was the prejudice against the prediction of new particles that theorists as eminent as Danish physicist Niels Bohr preferred to suggest that the law of conservation of energy might break down at subnuclear distances.

By 1935, however, Pauli's new particle had found a champion in Enrico Fermi. Fermi named the particle the neutrino and incorporated it into his theory for beta decay, published in 1934. Like Yukawa, Fermi drew on an analogy with QED. But Fermi regarded the emission of the neutrino and electron by the neutron as the direct analog of the emission of a photon by a charged particle, and he did not invoke a new exchange particle. Only later did it become clear that, strictly speaking, the neutron emits an antineutrino.

Fermi's theory, rather than Yukawa's, proved highly successful in describing nuclear beta decay, and it received added support in the late 1940s with the discovery of the pion and its relationship with the muon. In particular, the muon decays to an electron, a neutrino, and an antineutrino in a process that has exactly the same basic strength as the neutron's decay to a proton. The idea of a "universal" weak interaction that, unlike the strong force, acts equally upon light and heavy particles (or leptons and hadrons) was born.

EARLY THEORIES

The nature of the weak force began to be further revealed in 1956 as the result of work by two Chinese American theorists, Tsung-Dao Lee and Chen Ning Yang. Lee and Yang were trying to resolve some puzzles in the decays of the strange particles. They discovered that they could solve the mystery, provided that the weak force does not respect the symmetry known as parity.

The parity operation is like reflecting something in a mirror. It involves changing the coordinates (x, y, z) of each point to the "mirror" coordinates $(-x, -y, -z)$. In general, if a system is identical to the original system after a parity transformation, the system is said to have even parity. If the final formulation is the negative of the original, its parity is odd. For either parity the physical observables, which depend on the square of the wave function, are unchanged. A complex system has an overall parity that is the product of the parities of its components. Physicists had always assumed that such an operation would make no difference to the laws of physics.

It was assumed that, when an isolated system of fundamental particles interacts, the overall parity remains the same or is conserved. This conservation of parity implied that, for fundamental physical interactions, it is impossible to distinguish right from left and clockwise from counterclockwise. The laws of physics, it was thought, are indifferent to mirror reflection and could never predict a change in parity of a system. This law of the conservation of parity was explicitly formulated in the early 1930s by the Hungarian-born physicist Eugene P. Wigner and became an intrinsic part of quantum mechanics.

The fundamental laws governing the weak force should not be indifferent to mirror reflection, and, therefore, particle interactions that occur by means of the weak force should show some measure of built-in right- or left-handedness that might be experimentally detectable. In 1957 a team led by the Chinese-born physicist Chien-Shiung Wu announced conclusive experimental proof that the electrons ejected along with antineutrinos from certain unstable cobalt nuclei in the process of beta decay, a weak interaction, are predominantly left-handed—that is to say, the spin rotation of the electrons is that of a left-handed screw. Later that year Lee and Yang were awarded the Nobel Prize for Physics for their work. Nevertheless, it is believed on strong theoretical grounds (i.e., the CPT theorem) that when the operation of parity reversal P is joined with two others, called charge conjugation C and time reversal T, the combined operation does leave the fundamental laws unchanged.

Parity violation and the concept of a universal form of weak interaction were combined into one theory in 1958 by the American physicists Murray Gell-Mann and Richard Feynman. They established the mathematical structure of the weak interaction in what is known as V-A, or vector minus axial vector, theory. This theory proved highly successful experimentally, at least at the relatively low energies accessible to particle physicists in the 1960s. It was clear that the theory had the correct kind of mathematical structure to account for parity violation and related effects, but there were strong indications that, in describing particle interactions at higher energies than experiments could at the time access, the theory began to go badly wrong.

The problems with V-A theory were related to a basic requirement of quantum field theory—the existence of a gauge boson, or messenger particle, to carry the force. Yukawa had attempted to describe the weak force in terms of the same intermediary that is responsible for the nuclear binding force, but this approach did not work. A few years after Yukawa published his theory, a Swedish theorist, Oskar Klein, proposed a slightly different kind of carrier for the weak force.

In contrast to Yukawa's particle, which had spin 0, Klein's intermediary had spin 1 and therefore would give the correct spins for the antineutrino and the electron emitted in the beta decay of the neutron. Moreover, within the framework of Klein's concept, the known strength of the weak force in beta decay showed that the mass of the particle must be approximately 100 times the proton's mass, although the theory could not predict this value. All attempts to introduce such a particle into V-A theory, however, encountered severe difficulties, similar to those that had beset QED during the 1930s and early '40s. The theory gave infinite probabilities to various interactions, and it defied the renormalization process that had been the salvation of QED.

The discovery that the weak force conserves neither charge conjugation nor parity separately, however, led to a quantitative theory establishing combined CP as a symmetry of nature. Physicists reasoned that if CP were invariant, time reversal T would have to remain so as well. But further experiments, carried out in 1964 by a team led by the American physicists James W. Cronin and Val Logsdon Fitch, demonstrated that the electrically neutral K-meson—which normally decays via the weak force to give three pi-mesons—decayed a fraction of the time into only two such particles and thereby violated CP symmetry. CP violation implied nonconservation of T, provided that the long-held CPT theorem was valid. The CPT theorem, regarded as one of the basic principles of quantum field theory, states that all interactions should be invariant under the combined application of charge conjugation, parity, and time reversal in any order. CPT symmetry is an exact symmetry of all fundamental interactions.

The theoretical description of subatomic particles and forces known as the Standard Model contains an explanation of CP violation, but, as the effects of the phenomenon are small, it has proved difficult to show conclusively that this explanation is correct. The root of the effect lies in the weak force between quarks, the particles that make up K-mesons. The weak force appears to act not upon a pure quark state, as identified by the "flavour" or type of quark, but on a quantum mixture of two types of quarks. In 1972 the Japanese theoretical physicists Kobayashi Makoto and Maskawa Toshihide proposed that CP violation would be an inherent prediction of the Standard Model of particle physics if there were six types of quarks. (In 2008 Kobayashi and Maskawa were awarded the Nobel Prize for Physics for their "discovery of the origin of the broken symmetry which predicts the existence of at least three families of quarks in nature.") They realized that with six types of quarks, quantum mixing would allow very rare decays that would violate CP symmetry. Their predictions were borne out by the discovery of the third generation of quarks, the bottom and top quarks, in 1977 and 1995, respectively.

Experiments with neutral K-mesons appear to confirm detailed predictions of the Kobayashi-Maskawa theory, but the effects are very small. CP violation is expected to be more prominent in the decay of the particles known as B-mesons, which contain a bottom quark instead of the strange quark of the K-mesons. Experiments at facilities that can produce large numbers of the B-mesons (which are heavier than the K-mesons) are continuing to test these ideas. In 2010 scientists at the Fermi National

Accelerator Laboratory in Batavia, Ill., finally detected a slight preference for B-mesons to decay into muons rather than anti-muons.

CP violation has important theoretical consequences. The violation of CP symmetry enables physicists to make an absolute distinction between matter and anti-matter. The distinction between matter and antimatter may have profound implications for cosmology. One of the unsolved theoretical questions in physics is why the universe is made chiefly of matter. With a series of debatable but plausible assumptions, it can be demon-strated that the observed imbalance or asymmetry in the matter-antimatter ratio may have been produced by the occurrence of CP violation in the first seconds after the big bang—the violent explosion that is thought to have resulted in the formation of the universe.

HIDDEN SYMMETRY

Throughout the 1950s, theorists tried to construct field theories for the nuclear forces that would exhibit the same kind of gauge symmetry inherent in James Clerk Maxwell's theory of electrodynamics and in QED. There were two major problems, which were in fact related. One concerned the infinities and the difficulty in renormaliz-ing these theories. The other concerned the mass of the intermediaries. Straightforward gauge theory requires particles of zero mass as carriers, such as the photon of QED, but Klein had shown that the short-ranged weak force requires massive carriers.

Valid symmetry operations are those that can be per-formed without changing the appearance of an object. The number and type of such operations depend on the geom-etry of the object to which the operations are applied. The meaning and variety of symmetry operations may be illustrated by considering a square lying on a table. For the square, valid operations are (1) rotation about its centre through 90°, 180°, 270°, or 360°; (2) reflection through mirror planes perpendicular to the table and running either through any two opposite corners of the square or through the midpoints of any two opposing sides; and (3) reflection through a mirror plane in the plane of the table. Therefore there are nine symmetry operations that yield a result indistinguishable from the original square. A circle would be said to have higher symmetry because, for example, it could be rotated through an infinite number of angles (not just multiples of 90°) to give an identical circle.

Subatomic particles have various properties and are affected by certain forces that exhibit symmetry. An important property that gives rise to a conservation law is parity. In quantum mechanics all elementary particles and atoms may be described in terms of a wave equation. If this wave equation remains identical after simultaneous reflection of all spatial coordinates of the particle through the origin of the coordinate system, then it is said to have even parity. If such simultaneous reflection results in a wave equation that differs from the original wave equation only in sign, the particle is said to have odd parity. The overall parity of a collection of particles, such as a molecule, is found to be unchanged with time during physical processes and reactions. This fact is expressed as the law of conservation of parity. At the subatomic level, however, parity is not conserved in reactions that are caused by the weak force.

Elementary particles are also said to have internal symmetry. These symmetries are useful in classifying particles and in leading to selection rules. Such an internal symmetry is baryon number, which is a property of a class of particles called hadrons. Hadrons with a baryon number of zero are called mesons, those with a number of +1 are baryons. By symmetry there must exist another class of particles with a baryon number of -1. These are the antimatter counterparts of baryons called antibaryons. Baryon number is conserved during nuclear interactions.

In short, physicists had to discover the correct mathematical symmetry group for describing the transformations between different subatomic particles and then identify for the known forces the messenger particles required by fields with the chosen symmetry. Early in the 1960s Sheldon Glashow in the United States and Abdus Salam and John Ward in England decided to work with a combination of two symmetry groups—namely, $SU(2) \times U(1)$. Such a symmetry requires four spin-1 messenger particles, two electrically neutral and two charged. One of the neutral particles could be identified with the photon, while the two charged particles could be the messengers responsible for beta decay, in which charge changes hands, as when the neutron decays into a proton. The fourth messenger, a second neutral particle, seemed at the time to have no obvious role. It apparently would permit weak interactions with no change of charge— so-called neutral current interactions—which had not yet been observed.

This theory, however, still required the messengers to be massless, which was all right for the photon but not for the messengers of the weak force. Toward the end of the 1960s, Salam and Steven Weinberg, an American theorist, independently realized how to introduce massive messenger particles into the theory while at the same time preserving its basic gauge symmetry properties. The answer lay in the work of the English theorist Peter Higgs and others, who had discovered the concept of symmetry breaking, or, more descriptively, hidden symmetry.

A physical field can be intrinsically symmetrical, although this may not be apparent in the state of the universe in which experiments are conducted. On the Earth's surface, for example, gravity seems asymmetrical—it always pulls down. From a distance, however, the symmetry of the gravitational field around the Earth becomes apparent. At a more fundamental level, the fields associated with the electromagnetic and weak forces are not overtly symmetrical, as is demonstrated by the widely differing strengths of weak and electromagnetic interactions at low energies. Yet, according to Higgs's ideas, these forces can have an underlying symmetry. It is as if the universe lies at the bottom of a wine bottle. The symmetry of the bottle's base is clear from the top of the dimple in the centre, but it is hidden from any point in the valley surrounding the central dimple.

Higgs's mechanism for symmetry breaking provided Salam and Weinberg with a means of explaining the masses of the carriers of the weak force. Their theory, however, also predicted the existence of one or more new "Higgs"

To illustrate Higgs's postulation that electromagnetic and weak forces can have an underlying symmetry, imagine the universe at the base of a wine bottle: the symmetry of the bottle's base is obvious from the dimple's top but not from anywhere in the surrounding valley. Jupiterimages/Polka Dot/Thinkstock particles, which would carry additional fields needed for the symmetry breaking and would have spin 0. With this sole proviso the future of the electroweak theory began to look more promising. In 1971 a young Dutch theorist, Gerardus 't Hooft, building on work by Martinus Veltmann, proved that the theory is renormalizable (in other words, that all the infinities cancel out). Many particle physicists became convinced that the electroweak theory was, at last, an acceptable theory for the weak force.

FINDING THE MESSENGER PARTICLES

In addition to the Higgs particle, or particles, electroweak theory also predicts the existence of an electrically neutral carrier for the weak force. This neutral carrier, called the Z°, should mediate the neutral current interactions—weak interactions in which electric charge is not transferred between particles. The search for evidence of such reactions, which would confirm the validity of the electroweak theory, began in earnest in the early 1970s.

The first signs of neutral currents came in 1973 from experiments at the European Organization for Nuclear Research (CERN) near Geneva. A team of more than 50 physicists from a variety of countries had diligently searched through the photographs taken of tracks produced when a large bubble chamber called Gargamelle was exposed to a beam of muon-antineutrinos. In a neutral current reaction an antineutrino would simply scatter from an electron in the liquid contents of the bubble chamber. The incoming antineutrino, being neutral, would leave no track, nor would it leave a track as it left the chamber after being scattered off an electron. But the effect of the neutral current—the passage of a virtual Z° between the antineutrino and the electron—would set the electron in motion, and, being electrically charged, the electron would leave a track, which would appear as if from nowhere. Examining approximately 1.4 million pictures, the researchers found three examples of such a neutral current reaction. Although the reactions occurred only rarely, there were enough to set hopes high for the validity of electroweak theory.

In 1979 Glashow, Salam, and Weinberg, the theorists who had done much of the work in developing electroweak theory in the 1960s, were awarded the Nobel Prize for Physics; 't Hooft and Veltmann were similarly rewarded in 1999. By that time, enough information on charged and neutral current interactions had been compiled to predict that the masses of the weak messengers required by electroweak theory should be about 80 gigaelectron volts (GeV; 10^9 eV) for the charged W^+ and W^- particles and 90 GeV for the Z°.

In low-energy processes such as radioactive beta decay, the heavy W particles can be exchanged only because the uncertainty principle in quantum mechanics allows fluctuations in mass-energy over sufficiently short timescales. Such W particles can never be observed directly. However, detectable W particles can be produced in particle-accelerator experiments involving collisions between subatomic particles, provided that the collision energy is high enough. A W particle of this kind then decays into a charged lepton (e.g., electron, muon, or tau) and an associated neutrino or into a quark and an antiquark of different type (or "flavour") but with a total charge of +1 or -1. There was, however, in 1979 still no sign of the direct production of the weak messengers, because no accelerator was yet capable of producing collisions energetic enough to create real particles of such large masses (nearly 100 times as massive as the proton).

A scheme to find the W and Z particles was under way at CERN, however. The plan was to accelerate protons in one direction around CERN's largest proton synchrotron (a circular accelerator) and antiprotons in the opposite direction. At an appropriate energy (initially 270 GeV per beam), the two sets of particles would be made to collide head-on. The total energy of the collision would be far greater than anything that could be achieved by directing a single beam at a stationary target, and physicists hoped it would be sufficient to produce a small but significant number of W and Z particles.

In 1983 the researchers at CERN, working on two experiments code-named UA1 and UA2, were rewarded with the discovery of the particles they sought. The Ws and Zs that were produced did not live long enough to leave tracks in the detectors, but they decayed to particles that did leave tracks. The total energy of those decay particles, moreover, equaled the energy corresponding to the masses of the transient W and Z particles, just as predicted by electroweak theory. It was a triumph both for CERN and for electroweak theory. Hundreds of physicists and engineers were involved in the project, and in 1984 the Italian physicist Carlo Rubbia and Dutch engineer Simon van der Meer received the Nobel Prize for Physics for their leading roles in making the discovery of the W and Z particles possible.

The W particles play a crucial role in interactions that turn one flavour of quark or lepton into another, as in the beta decay of a neutron, where a down quark turns into an up quark to form a proton. Such flavour-changing interactions occur only through the weak force and are described by the SU(2) symmetry that underlies electroweak theory along with U(1). The basic representation of this mathematical group is a pair, or doublet, and, according to electroweak theory, the quarks and leptons are each grouped into pairs of increasing mass: (u, d), (c, s), (t, b) and (e, v_e), (μ, v_μ), (τ, v_τ). This underlying symmetry does not, however, indicate how many pairs of quarks and leptons should exist in total. This question was answered in experiments at CERN in 1989, when the colliding-beam storage ring particle accelerator known as the Large Electron-Positron (LEP) collider came into operation.

Since that time LEP has been used to produce thousands of Z particles by colliding electrons and positrons at total energies of about 92 GeV. Studies of the decay of the Z particles produced in this way reveal what is known as the "width" of the Z, or the intrinsic variation in its mass. This width is related to the particle's lifetime through the uncertainty principle, which states that the shorter the lifetime of a quantum state, the greater the uncertainty in its energy or, equivalently, its mass. The width of the Z particle thus gives a measure of its lifetime and thereby reflects the number of ways in which the particle can decay, since the greater the number of ways it can decay, the shorter its life. In particular, measurements at CERN show that when the Z decays to neutrino-antineutrino pairs, it produces three and only three types of lightweight neutrino. This measurement is of fundamental importance because it indicates that there are only three sets each of leptons and quarks, the basic building blocks of matter.

Since the early work at CERN, W particles have been generated in much greater numbers in the 1,800-GeV Tevatron proton-antiproton collider at the Fermi National Accelerator Laboratory and in the Large Electron-Positron collider at CERN. These experiments have yielded more precise measurements of the mass of the W particle, now known to be close to 80.4 GeV.

CURRENT RESEARCH IN PARTICLE PHYSICS

Particle physics has evolved and continues to evolve. Refined measurements can reveal unexpected behaviour. Conversely, mathematical extrapolation of existing theories into new theoretical areas, critical reexamination of apparently obvious but untested assumptions, argument by symmetry or analogy, aesthetic judgment, pure accident, and hunch each plays a role (as in all of science).

EXPERIMENTS

Electroweak theory, which describes the electromagnetic and weak forces, and quantum chromodynamics, the gauge theory of the strong force, together form what particle physicists call the Standard Model. The Standard Model, which provides an organizing framework for the classification of all known subatomic particles, works well as far as can be measured by means of present technology, but several points still await experimental verification or clarification. Furthermore, the model is still incomplete.

TESTING THE STANDARD MODEL

Prior to 1994 one of the main missing ingredients of the Standard Model was the top quark, which was required to complete the set of three pairs of quarks. Searches for this sixth and heaviest quark failed repeatedly until in April 1994 a team working on the Collider Detector Facility (CDF) at Fermi National Accelerator Laboratory (Fermilab) in Batavia, Ill., announced tentative evidence for the top quark. This was confirmed the following year, when not only the CDF team but also an independent team working on a second experiment at Fermilab, code-named DZero, or D0, published more convincing evidence. The results indicated that the top quark has a mass between 170 and 190 gigaelectron volts (GeV; 10^9 eV). This is almost as heavy as a nucleus of lead, so it was not surprising that previous experiments had failed to find the top quark. The discovery had required the highest-energy particle collisions available—those at Fermilab's Tevatron, which collides protons with antiprotons at a total energy of 1,800 GeV, or 1.8 teraelectron volts (TeV; 10^{12} eV). The discovery of the top quark in a sense completed another chapter in the history of particle physics. It also focused the attention of experimenters on other questions unanswered by the Standard Model. For instance, why are there six quarks and not more or less? It may be that only this number of quarks allows for the subtle difference between particles and antiparticles that occurs in the neutral K mesons ($K°$ and $\bar{K}°$), which contain an s quark (or antiquark) bound with a d antiquark (or quark). This asymmetry between particle and antiparticle could in turn be related to the domination of matter over antimatter in the universe. Experiments studying neutral B mesons, which contain a b quark or its antiquark, may eventually reveal similar effects and so cast light on this fundamental problem that links particle physics with cosmology and the study of the origin of matter in the universe.

TESTING SUPERSYMMETRY

A physical entity is said to exhibit symmetry when it appears unchanged after undergoing a transformation operation. A square, for example, has a fourfold symmetry by which it appears the same when rotated about its centre through 90, 180, 270, and 360 degrees. Four 90-degree rotations bring the square back to its original position. Symmetry with respect to time and space transformations is embodied within physical laws such as the conservation of energy and the conservation of momentum. With supersymmetry, fermions can be transformed into bosons without changing the structure of the underlying theory of the particles and their interactions. Thus, supersymmetry provides a relationship between the elementary particles that make up matter—quarks and leptons, which are all fermions—and the "force-carrier" particles that transmit the fundamental interactions of matter (all bosons). By showing that one type of particle is in effect a different facet of the other type, supersymmetry reduces the number of basic types of particle from two to one.

When a fermion is transformed into a boson and then back again into a fermion, it turns out that the particle has moved in space, an effect that is related to special relativity. Supersymmetry therefore relates transformations in an internal property of particles (spin) to transformations in space-time. In particular, when supersymmetry is made a "local" symmetry, so that the transformations vary over space-time, it automatically includes a particle with a spin of 2, which can be identified as the graviton, the "force carrier" associated with gravity. Theories involving supersymmetry in its local form are therefore often known as supergravity theories.

Theories of supergravity have developed out of attempts to construct a unified field theory that would describe all of the four basic forces. One of the essential features of a quantum field theory is its prediction of "force-carrier" particles that are exchanged between interacting particles of matter. It is in this context that the gravitational force has proved difficult to treat as a quantum field theory. General relativity, which relates the gravitational force to the curvature of space-time, provides a respectable theory of gravity on a larger scale. To be consistent with general relativity, gravity at the quantum level must be carried by a particle, called the graviton, with an intrinsic angular momentum (spin) of 2 units—in contrast to the other fundamental forces, whose carrier particles (e.g., the photon and the gluon) have a spin of 1.

A particle with the properties of the graviton appears naturally in certain theories based on supersymmetry—a symmetry that relates fermions (particles with half-integer values of spin) and bosons (particles with integer values of spin). In these theories supersymmetry is treated as a "local" symmetry. In other words, its transformations vary over space-time. Treating supersymmetry in this way relates it to general relativity, and so gravity is automatically included. Moreover, supergravity theories are more likely to be free from various inconsistent or "nonphysical" infinite quantities that usually arise in calculations involving quantum theories of gravity. These "infinities" are canceled by the effects of the additional particles that supersymmetry predicts (every particle must have a supersymmetric partner with the other type of spin).

Supergravity theories permit extra dimensions in space-time, beyond the familiar three dimensions of space and one of time. Supergravity models in higher dimensions "reduce" to the familiar four-dimensional space-time if it is postulated that the extra dimensions are compacted or curled up in such a way that they are not noticeable. An analogy would be a three-dimensional pipe that appears as a one-dimensional line from a distance because two dimensions are curled up as a small circle. The advantage of the extra dimensions is that they allow supergravity theories to incorporate the electromagnetic, weak, and strong forces as well as gravity. The maximum number of dimensions allowed in the theories is 11, and there are indications that a viable and unique unified theory that describes all particles and forces may be based in 11 dimensions. Such a theory would subsume the superstring theories in 10 dimensions, which first offered the promise of a self-consistent and fully unified "theory of everything" in the 1980s.

Much of current research, meanwhile, is centred on important precision tests that may reveal effects due to supersymmetry. These studies include measurements based on millions of Z particles produced in the LEP collider at the European Organization for Nuclear Research (CERN) and in the Stanford Linear Collider (SLC) at the

Stanford Linear Accelerator Center (SLAC) in Menlo Park, Calif., and on large numbers of W particles produced in the Tevatron synchrotron at Fermilab and later at the LEP collider. The precision of these measurements is such that comparisons with the predictions of the Standard Model constrain the allowed range of values for quantities that are otherwise unknown. The predictions depend, for example, on the mass of the top quark, and in this case comparison with the precision measurements indicates a value in good agreement with the mass measured at Fermilab. This agreement makes another comparison all the more interesting, for the precision data also provide hints as to the mass of the Higgs particle—a major ingredient of the Standard Model that has yet to be discovered.

The Higgs particle is the particle associated with the mechanism that allows the symmetry of the electroweak force to be broken, or hidden, at low energies and that gives the W and Z particles, the carriers of the weak force, their mass. The particle is necessary to electroweak theory because the Higgs mechanism requires a new field to break the symmetry, and, according to quantum field theory, all fields have particles associated with them. Theory provides a poor guide as to the particle's mass or even the number of different varieties of Higgs particles involved. However, comparisons with the precision measurements from the LEP collider suggest that the mass of the Higgs particle may be quite light, perhaps less than 200 GeV, although the data do not rule out a much heavier Higgs particle with a mass greater than 1 TeV.

The hypothetical Higgs particle (or Higgs boson) is postulated to be the carrier particle, or boson, of the Higgs field, a theoretical field that permeates space and endows all elementary subatomic particles with mass through its interactions with them. The field and the particle—named after Peter Higgs of the University of Edinburgh, one of the physicists who first proposed this mechanism—provide a testable hypothesis for the origin of mass in elementary particles. In popular culture, the Higgs particle is often called the "God particle," after the title of Nobel physicist Leon Lederman's *The God Particle: If the Universe Is the Answer, What Is the Question?* (1993), which contained the author's assertion that the discovery of the particle is crucial to a final understanding of the structure of matter.

The Higgs field is different from other fundamental fields—such as the electromagnetic field—that underlie the basic forces between particles. First, it is a scalar field (i.e., it has magnitude but no direction). This implies that its carrier, the Higgs boson, has an intrinsic angular momentum, or spin, of 0, unlike the carriers of the force fields, which have spin. Second, the Higgs field has the unusual property that its energy is higher when the field is zero than when it is nonzero. The elementary particles therefore acquired their masses through interactions with a nonzero Higgs field only when the universe cooled and became less energetic in the aftermath of the big bang (the hypothetical primal explosion in which the universe originated). The variety of masses characterizing the elementary subatomic particles arises because different particles have different strengths of interaction with the Higgs field.

Further new particles are predicted by theories that include supersymmetry. This symmetry relates quarks and leptons, which have spin ½ and are collectively called fermions, with the bosons of the gauge fields, which have spins 1 or 2, and with the Higgs particle, which has spin 0. This symmetry appeals to theorists in particular because it allows them to bring together all the particles—quarks, leptons, and gauge bosons—in theories that unite the various forces. The price to pay is a doubling of the number of fundamental particles, as the new symmetry implies that the known particles all have supersymmetric counterparts with different spin. Thus, the leptons and quarks with spin ½ have super-symmetric partners, dubbed sleptons and squarks, with integer spin. The photon, W, Z, gluon, and graviton have counterparts with half-integer spins, known as the photino, wino, zino, gluino, and gravitino, respectively.

If they indeed exist, all these new supersymmetric particles must be heavy to have escaped detection so far. Theory suggests that some of the lightest of them could be created in collisions at the particle accelerators with the highest energies—that is, at the Tevatron and at the Hadron-Electron Ring Accelerator (HERA) at the DESY (German Electron Synchrotron) laboratory in Hamburg, Germany. Experiments at HERA and at the Tevatron also hold the promise of revealing any substructure within quarks or electrons. There is still a chance of more dis-coveries, including that of one or more Higgs particles, at the Large Hadron Collider, which began test operations at CERN in 2008. This machine, which was built in the same tunnel that housed the LEP collider until 2000, is designed to collide protons at energies of 7 TeV per beam.

INVESTIGATING NEUTRINOS

Other hints of physics beyond the present Standard Model concern the neutrinos. In the Standard Model these par-ticles have zero mass, so any measurement of a nonzero mass, however small, would indicate the existence of pro-cesses that are outside the Standard Model. Experiments to measure directly the masses of the three neutrinos yield only limits. That is, they give no sign of a mass for the par-ticular neutrino type but do rule out any values above the smallest mass the experiments can measure. Other experi-ments attempt to measure neutrino mass indirectly by investigating whether neutrinos can change from one type to another. Such neutrino "oscillations"—a quantum phe-nomenon due to the wavelike nature of the particles—can occur only if there is a difference in mass between the basic neutrino types.

The first indications that neutrinos might oscillate came from experiments to detect solar neutrinos. By the mid-1980s several different types of experiments, such as those conducted by the American physical chemist Raymond Davis, Jr., in a gold mine in South Dakota, had consistently observed only one-third to two-thirds the number of electron-neutrinos arriving at Earth from the Sun, where they are emitted by the nuclear reactions that convert hydrogen to helium in the solar core. A popular explanation was that the electron-neutrinos had changed to another type on their way through the Sun—for example, to muon-neutrinos. Muon-neutrinos would not have been detected by the original experiments, which were designed to capture electron-neutrinos. Then in 2002 the Sudbury Neutrino Observatory (SNO) in Ontario, Canada, announced the first direct evidence for neutrino oscillations in solar neutrinos. The experiment, which is based on 1,000 tons of heavy water, detects electron-neutrinos through one reaction, but it can also detect all types of neutrinos through another reaction. SNO finds that, while the number of neutrinos detected of any type is consistent with calculations based on the physics of the Sun's interior, the number of electron-neutrinos observed is about one-third the number expected. This implies that the "missing" electron-neutrinos have changed to one of the other types. According to theory, the amount of oscillation as neutrinos pass through matter (as in the Sun) depends on the difference between the squares of the masses of the basic neutrino types (which are in fact different from the observed electron-, muon-, and tau-neutrino "flavours"). Taking all available solar neutrino data together (as of 2002) and fitting them to a theoretical model based on oscillations between two basic types indicate a difference in the mass-squared of 5×10^{-5} eV^2.

Earlier evidence for neutrino oscillations came in 1998 from the Super-Kamiokande detector in the Kamioka Mine, Gifu prefecture, Japan, which was studying neutrinos created in cosmic-ray interactions on the opposite side of the Earth. The detector found fewer muon-neutrinos relative to electron-neutrinos coming up through the Earth than coming down through the atmosphere. This suggested the possibility that, as they travel through the Earth, muon-neutrinos change to tau-neutrinos, which could not be detected in Super-Kamiokande. These efforts won a Nobel Prize for Physics in 2002 for Super-Kamiokande's director, Koshiba Masatoshi. Davis was awarded a share of the prize for his earlier efforts in South Dakota.

Experiments at particle accelerators and nuclear reactors have found no conclusive evidence for oscillations over much-shorter distance scales, from tens to hundreds of metres. Since 2000 three "long-baseline" experiments have searched over longer distances of a few hundred kilometres for oscillations of muon-neutrinos created at accelerators. The aim is to build up a self-consistent picture that indicates clearly the values of neutrino masses.

LINKING TO THE COSMOS

Particle physics may supply the answer to what makes up dark matter, a component of the universe whose presence is discerned from its gravitational attraction rather than its luminosity. Dark matter makes up 26.5 percent of the matter-energy composition of the universe. The rest is dark energy (73 percent) and "ordinary" visible matter (0.5 percent).

Originally known as the "missing mass," dark matter's existence was first inferred by Swiss American astronomer Fritz Zwicky, who in 1933 discovered that the mass of all the stars in the Coma cluster of galaxies provided only about 1 percent of the mass needed to keep the galaxies from escaping the cluster's gravitational pull. The reality of this missing mass remained in question for decades, until the 1970s when American astronomers Vera Rubin and W. Kent Ford confirmed its existence by the observation of a similar phenomenon: the mass of the stars visible within a typical galaxy is only about 10 percent of that required to keep those stars orbiting the galaxy's centre. In general, the speed with which stars orbit the centre of their galaxy is independent of their separation from the centre. Indeed, orbital velocity is either constant or increases slightly with distance rather than dropping off as expected. To account for this, the mass of the galaxy within the orbit of the stars must increase linearly with the distance of the stars from the galaxy's centre. However, no light is seen from this inner mass—hence the name "dark matter."

Since the confirmation of dark matter's existence, a preponderance of dark matter in galaxies and clusters of galaxies has been discerned through the phenomenon of gravitational lensing—matter acting as a lens by bending space and distorting the passage of background light. The presence of this missing matter in the centres of galaxies and clusters of galaxies has also been inferred from the motion and heat of gas that gives rise to observed X-rays. For example, the Chandra X-ray Observatory has observed in the Bullet cluster, which consists of two merging galaxy clusters, that the hot gas (ordinary visible matter) is slowed by the drag effect of one cluster passing through the other. The mass of the clusters, however, is not affected, indicating that most of the mass consists of dark matter.

Twenty-seven percent of the universe's matter-energy composition is matter. Only 0.5 percent is in the mass of stars and 0.03 percent of that matter is in the form of elements heavier than hydrogen. The rest is dark matter. Two varieties of dark matter have been found to exist. The first variety is about 4.5 percent of the universe and is made of the familiar baryons (i.e., protons, neutrons, and atomic nuclei), which also make up the luminous stars and galaxies. Most of this baryonic dark matter is expected to exist in the form of gas in and between the galaxies. This baryonic, or ordinary, component of dark matter has been determined by measuring the abundance of elements heavier than hydrogen that were created in the first few minutes after the big bang that occurred 13.7 billion years ago.

The dark matter that comprises the other 22 percent of the universe's matter is in an unfamiliar, nonbaryonic form. The rate at which galaxies and large structures composed of galaxies coalesced from density fluctuations in the early universe indicates that the nonbaryonic dark matter is relatively "cold," or "nonrelativisitic," meaning that the backbones of galaxies and clusters of galaxies are made of heavy, slow-moving particles. The absence of light from these particles also indicates that they are electromagnetically neutral. These properties give rise to

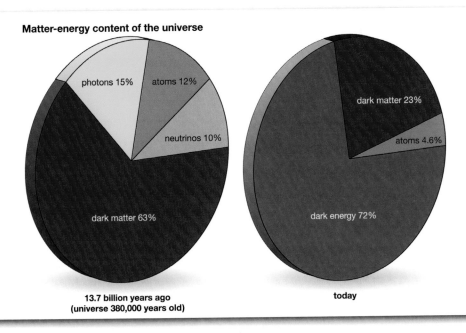

Matter-energy content of the universe

photons 15% atoms 12%

neutrinos 10%

dark matter 63%

dark matter 23%

atoms 4.6%

dark energy 72%

13.7 billion years ago
(universe 380,000 years old)

today

Matter-energy content of the universe. Encyclopædia Britannica, Inc.

the particles' common name, weakly interacting massive particles (WIMPs). If these particles were not massive and weakly interacting, they would already be known. The precise nature of these particles is not currently known, and they are not predicted by the standard model of particle physics. However, a number of possible extensions to the standard model such as supersymmetric theories predict hypothetical elementary particles such as axions or neutralinos that may be the undetected WIMPs.

Extraordinary efforts are under way to detect and measure the properties of these unseen WIMPs, either by witnessing their impact in a laboratory detector or by observing their annihilations after they collide with each other, as Earth moves through the dark matter that may exist in the Milky Way Galaxy. There is also some expectation that their presence and mass may be inferred from experiments at new particle accelerators such as the Large Hadron Collider.

As an alternative to dark matter, modifications to gravity have been proposed to explain the apparent presence of "missing matter." These modifications suggest that the attractive force exerted by ordinary matter may be enhanced in conditions that occur only on galactic scales. However, most of the proposals are unsatisfactory on theoretical grounds as they provide little or no explanation for the modification of gravity. These theories are also unable to explain the observations of dark matter physically separated from ordinary matter in the Bullet cluster. This separation demonstrates that dark matter is a physical reality and is distinguishable from ordinary matter.

Other current research involves the search for a new state of matter called the quark-gluon plasma. This should have existed for only 10 microseconds or so after the birth of the universe in the big bang, when the universe was too hot and energetic for quarks to coalesce

The mass and presence of WIMPs (weakly interacting massive particles) in the Milky Way Galaxy may be confirmed with experiments by particle accelerators such as the Large Hadron Collider. Fabrice Coffrini/AFP/ Getty Images

into particles such as neutrons and protons. The quarks, and the gluons through which they interact, should have existed freely as a plasma, akin to the more familiar plasma of ions and electrons that forms when conditions are too energetic for electrons to remain attached to atomic nuclei, as, for example, in the Sun. In experiments at CERN and at the Brookhaven National Laboratory in Upton, N.Y., physicists collide heavy nuclei at high energies in order to achieve temperatures and densities that may be high enough for the matter in the nuclei to change phase from the normal state, with quarks con-fined within protons and neutrons, to a plasma of free quarks and gluons. One way that this new state of mat-ter should reveal itself is through the creation of more strange quarks, and hence more strange particles, than in normal collisions. CERN has claimed to have observed hints of quark-gluon plasma, but clear evidence will come only from experiments at the Relativistic Heavy Ion Collider (RHIC) at Brookhaven and the Large Hadron Collider at CERN. These experiments, together with those that search for particles of dark matter and those that investigate the differences between matter and anti-matter, illustrate the growing interdependence between particle physics and cosmology—the sciences of the very small and the very large.

THEORY

Electroweak theory allows extremely precise calculations to be made. However, problems arise with the theory of the strong force, quantum chromodynamics (QCD), despite its similar structure as a gauge theory.

LIMITS OF QUANTUM CHROMODYNAMICS AND THE STANDARD MODEL

At short distances or equivalently high energies, the effects of the strong force become weaker. This means that complex interactions between quarks, involving many gluon exchanges, become highly improbable, and the basic interactions can be calculated from relatively few exchanges, just as in electroweak theory. As the distance between quarks increases, however, the increasing effect of the strong force means that the multiple interactions must be taken into account, and the calculations quickly become intractable. The outcome is that it is difficult to calculate the properties of hadrons, in particular their masses, which depend on the energy tied up in the interactions between the quarks they contain.

Since the 1980s, however, the advent of supercomputers with increased processing power has enabled theorists to make some progress in calculations that are based on a lattice of points in space-time. This is clearly an approximation to the continuously varying space-time of the real gauge theory, but it reduces the amount of calculation required. The greater the number of points in the lattice, the better the approximation. The computation times involved are still long, even for the most powerful computers available, but theorists are beginning to have some success in calculating the masses of hadrons from the underlying interactions between the quarks.

Meanwhile, the Standard Model combining electroweak theory and quantum chromodynamics provides a satisfactory way of understanding most experimental results in particle physics, yet it is far from satisfying as a theory. In addition to the missing Higgs particle, many problems and gaps in the model have been explained in a rather ad hoc manner. Values for such basic properties as the fractional charges of quarks or the masses of quarks and leptons must be inserted "by hand" into the model—that is, they are determined by experiment and observation rather than by theoretical predictions.

TOWARD A GRAND UNIFIED THEORY

Many theorists working in particle physics are therefore looking beyond the Standard Model in an attempt to find a more comprehensive theory. One important approach has been the development of grand unified theories, or GUTs, which seek to unify the strong, weak, and electromagnetic forces in the way that electroweak theory does for two of these forces.

Such theories were initially inspired by evidence that the strong force is weaker at shorter distances or, equivalently, at higher energies. This suggests that at a sufficiently high energy the strengths of the weak, electromagnetic, and strong interactions may become the same, revealing an underlying symmetry between the forces that is hidden at lower energies. This symmetry must incorporate the symmetries of both QCD and electroweak theory, which are manifest at lower energies. There are various possibilities, but the simplest and most-studied GUTs are based on the mathematical symmetry group SU(5).

As all GUTs link the strong interactions of quarks with the electroweak interactions between quarks and leptons, they generally bring the quarks and leptons together into the overall symmetry group. This implies that a quark can convert into a lepton (and vice versa), which in turn leads to the conclusion that protons, the lightest stable particles built from quarks, are not in fact stable but can decay to lighter leptons. These interactions between quarks and leptons occur through new gauge bosons, generally called X, which must have masses comparable to the energy scale of grand unification. The mean life for the proton, according to the GUTs, depends on this mass. In the simplest GUTs based on SU(5), the mean life varies as the fourth power of the mass of the X boson.

Experimental results, principally from the LEP collider at CERN, suggest that the strengths of the strong, weak, and electromagnetic interactions should converge at energies of about 10^{16} GeV. This tremendous mass means that proton decay should occur only rarely, with a mean life of about 10^{35} years. (This result is fortunate, as protons must be stable on timescales of at least 10^{17} years. Otherwise, all matter would be measurably radioactive.) It might seem that verifying such a lifetime experimentally would be impossible. However, particle lifetimes are only averages. Given a large-enough collection of protons, there is a chance that a few may decay within an observable time. This encouraged physicists in the 1980s to set up a number of proton-decay experiments in which large quantities of inexpensive material—usually water, iron, or concrete—were surrounded by detectors that could spot the particles produced should a proton decay. Such experiments confirmed that the proton lifetime must be greater than 10^{32} years, but detectors capable of measuring a lifetime of 10^{35} years have yet to be established.

The experimental results from the LEP collider also provide clues about the nature of a realistic GUT. The detailed extrapolation from the LEP collider's energies of about 100 GeV to the grand unification energies of about 10^{16} GeV depends on the particular GUT used in making the extrapolation. It turns out that, for the strengths of the strong, weak, and electromagnetic interactions to converge properly, the GUT must include supersymmetry—the symmetry between fermions (quarks and leptons) and the gauge bosons that mediate their interactions. Supersymmetry, which predicts that every known particle should have a partner with different spin, also has the attraction of relieving difficulties that arise with the masses of particles, particularly in GUTs. The problem in a GUT is that all particles, including the quarks and leptons, tend to acquire masses of about 10^{16} GeV, the unification energy. The introduction of the additional particles required by supersymmetry helps by canceling out other contributions that lead to the high masses and thus leaves the quarks and leptons with the masses measured in experiment. This important effect has led to the strong conviction among theorists that supersymmetry should be found in nature, although evidence for the supersymmetric particles has yet to be found.

A THEORY OF EVERYTHING

While GUTs resolve some of the problems with the Standard Model, they remain inadequate in a number of respects. They give no explanation, for example, for the number of pairs of quarks and leptons. They even raise the question of why such an enormous gap exists between the masses of the W and Z bosons of the electroweak force and the X bosons of lepton-quark interactions. Most important, they do not include the fourth force, gravity.

The dream of theorists is to find a totally unified theory—a theory of everything, or TOE. Attempts to derive a quantum field theory containing gravity always ran aground, however, until a remarkable development in 1984 first hinted that a quantum theory that includes gravity might be possible. The new development brought together two ideas that originated in the 1970s. One was supersymmetry, with its abilities to remove nonphysical infinite values from theories. The other was string theory, which regards all particles—quarks, leptons, and bosons—not as points in space, as in conventional field theories, but as extended one-dimensional objects, or "strings."

The incorporation of supersymmetry with string theory is known as superstring theory, and its importance was recognized in the mid-1980s when an English theorist, Michael Green, and an American theoretical physicist, John Schwarz, showed that in certain cases superstring theory is entirely self-consistent. All potential problems cancel out, despite the fact that the theory requires a massless particle of spin 2—in other words, the gauge boson of gravity, the graviton—and thus automatically contains a quantum description of gravity. It soon seemed, however, that there were many superstring theories that included gravity, and this appeared to undermine the claim that superstrings would yield a single theory of everything. In the late 1980s new ideas emerged concerning two-dimensional membranes or higher-dimensional "branes," rather than strings, that also encompass supergravity. Among the many efforts to resolve these seemingly disparate treatments of superstring space in a coherent and consistent manner was that of Edward Witten of the Institute for Advanced Study in Princeton, N.J. Witten proposed that the existing superstring theories are actually limits of a more-general underlying 11-dimensional "M-theory" that offers the promise of a self-consistent quantum treatment of all particles and forces.

STRING THEORY

String theory attempts to merge quantum mechanics with Albert Einstein's general theory of relativity. The name *string theory* comes from the modeling of subatomic particles as tiny one-dimensional "stringlike" entities rather than the more conventional approach in which they are modeled as zero-dimensional point particles. The theory envisions that a string undergoing a particular mode of vibration corresponds to a particle with definite properties such as mass and charge. In the 1980s, physicists realized that string theory had the potential to incorporate all four of nature's forces—gravity, electromagnetism, strong force, and weak force—and all types of matter in a single quantum mechanical framework, suggesting that it might be the long-sought unified field theory. While string theory is still a vibrant area of research that is undergoing rapid development, it remains a purely mathematical construct because it has yet to make contact with experimental observations.

In 1905 Einstein unified space and time with his special theory of relativity, showing that motion through space affects the passage of time. In 1915 Einstein further unified space, time, and gravitation with his general theory of relativity, showing that warps and curves in space and time are responsible for the force of gravity. These were monumental achievements, but Einstein dreamed of an even grander unification. He envisioned one powerful framework that would account for space, time, and all of nature's forces—something he called a unified theory. For the last three decades of his life, Einstein relentlessly pursued his quixotic vision. Although from time to time rumours spread that he had succeeded, closer scrutiny always dashed such hopes. Most of Einstein's contemporaries considered the search for a unified theory to be a hopeless, if not misguided, quest.

In contrast, the primary concern of theoretical physicists from the 1920s onward was quantum mechanics—the emerging framework for describing atomic and subatomic processes. Particles at these scales have such tiny masses that gravity is essentially irrelevant in their interactions, and so for decades quantum mechanical calculations generally ignored relativistic effects. Instead, by the late 1960s the focus was on a different force—the strong force, which binds together the protons and neutrons within atomic nuclei. Gabriele Veneziano, a young theorist working at the European Organization for Nuclear Research (CERN), contributed a key breakthrough in 1968 with his realization that a 200-year-old formula, the Euler beta function, was capable of explaining much of the data on the strong force then being collected at various particle accelerators around the world. A few years later, three physicists—Leonard Susskind of Stanford University, Holger Nielsen of the Niels Bohr Institute, and Yoichiro Nambu of the University of Chicago—significantly amplified Veneziano's insight by showing that the mathematics underlying his proposal described the vibrational motion of minuscule filaments of energy that resemble tiny strands of string, inspiring the name *string theory*. Roughly speaking, the theory suggested that the strong force amounted to strings tethering together particles attached to the strings' endpoints.

String theory was an intuitively attractive proposal, but by the mid-1970s more refined measurements of the strong force had deviated from its predictions, leading most researchers to conclude that string theory had no relevance to the physical universe, no matter how elegant the mathematical theory. Nevertheless, a small number of physicists continued to pursue string theory. In 1974 John Schwarz of the California Institute of Technology and Joel Scherk of the École Normale Supérieure and, independently, Tamiaki Yoneya of Hokkaido University came to a radical conclusion. They suggested that one of the supposedly failed predictions of string theory—the existence of a particular massless particle that no experiment studying the strong force had ever encountered—was actually evidence of the very unification Einstein had anticipated.

Although no one had succeeded in merging general relativity and quantum mechanics, preliminary work had established that such a union would require precisely the massless particle predicted by string theory. A few physicists argued that string theory, by having this particle built into its fundamental structure, had united the laws of the large (general relativity) and the laws of the small (quantum mechanics). Rather than merely being a description of the strong force, these physicists contended, string theory required reinterpretation as a critical step toward Einstein's unified theory.

The announcement was universally ignored. String theory had already failed in its first incarnation as a description of the strong force, and many felt it was unlikely that it would now prevail as the solution to an even more difficult problem. This view was bolstered by string theory's suffering from its own theoretical problems. For one, some of its equations showed signs of being inconsistent. For another, the mathematics of the theory demanded the universe have not just the three spatial dimensions of common experience but six others (for a total of nine spatial dimensions, or a total of ten space-time dimensions).

Because of these obstacles, the number of physicists working on the theory had dropped to two—Schwarz and Michael Green, of Queen Mary College, London—by the mid-1980s. But in 1984 these two die-hard string theorists achieved a major breakthrough. Through a remarkable calculation, they proved that the equations of string theory were consistent after all. By the time word of this result had spread throughout the physics community, hundreds of researchers had dropped what they were working on and turned their full attention to string theory.

Within a few months, string theory's unified framework took shape. Much as different vibrational patterns of a violin string play different musical notes, the different vibrations of the tiny strands in string theory were imagined to yield different particles of nature. According to the theory, the strings are so small that they appear to be points—as particles had long been thought to be—but in reality they have length (about 10^{-33} cm). The mass and charge of a particle is determined by how a string vibrates. For example, string theory posits that an electron is a string undergoing one particular vibrational pattern. A quark is imagined as a string undergoing a different vibrational pattern. Crucially, among the vibrational patterns, physicists argued, would also be the particles found by experiment to communicate nature's forces. Thus, string theory was proposed as the sought-for unification of all forces and all matter.

What of the six extra spatial dimensions required by string theory? Following a suggestion made in the 1920s by Theodor Kaluza of Germany and Oskar Klein of Sweden, string theorists envisioned that dimensions come in two distinct varieties. Like the unfurled length of a long garden hose, dimensions can be big and easy to see. But like the shorter, circular girth of the garden hose, dimensions can also be far smaller and more difficult to detect. This becomes more apparent by imagining that the circular cross section of the garden hose is shrunk ever smaller, below what can be seen with the naked eye,

Much more than mere points, particles are more like the strings on a violin, with mass and charge determined by the string's vibration. Don Emmert/ AFP/Getty Images

thereby misleading a casual observer into thinking the garden hose has only one dimension, its length. Similarly, according to string theory, the three dimensions of common experience are large and hence manifest, while the other six dimensions are crumpled so small that they have so far evaded detection.

During the decade from 1984 to 1994, many theoretical physicists strove to fulfill string theory's promise by developing this abstract, wholly mathematical framework into a concrete, predictive theory of nature. Because the infinitesimal size of strings has precluded their direct detection, theorists have sought to extract indirect implications of the theory that might be testable. In this regard, the extra dimensions of string theory have proved a major hurdle. Imagining these extra dimensions as small and hidden is a reasonable explanation for their apparent absence. However, also because strings are so small, they would vibrate in every dimension, not just in the usual three dimensions. Studies showed that, much as the shape and size of a French horn affect the vibrational patterns of airstreams coursing through the instrument, the exact shape and size of the extra dimensions would affect how strings vibrate. And since the strings' vibrations determine quantities such as particle masses and charges, predictivity requires knowledge of the geometrical form of the extra dimensions. Unfortunately, the equations of string theory allow the extra dimensions to take many different geometric forms, making it difficult to extract definitive testable predictions.

By the mid-1990s, these and other obstacles were again eroding the ranks of string theorists. But in 1995 another breakthrough reinvigorated the field. Edward Witten of the Institute for Advanced Study, building on contributions of many other physicists, proposed a new set of techniques that refined the approximate equations on which all work in string theory had so far been based. These techniques helped reveal a number of new features of string theory. Most dramatically, these more exact equations showed that string theory has not six but seven extra spatial dimensions. The more exact equations also revealed ingredients in string theory besides strings—membranelike objects of various dimensions, collectively called branes. Finally, the new techniques established that various versions of string theory developed over the preceding decades were essentially all the same. Theorists call this unification of formerly distinct string theories by a new name, M-theory, with the meaning of *M* being deferred until the theory is more fully understood.

Today, the understanding of many facets of string theory is still in its formative stage. Researchers recognize that, although remarkable progress has been made over the past three decades, collectively the work is burdened by its piecemeal development, with incremental discoveries having been joined like pieces of a jigsaw puzzle. That the pieces fit coherently is impressive, but the larger picture they are filling out—the fundamental principle underlying the theory—remains mysterious. Equally pressing, the theory has yet to be supported by observations and hence remains a totally theoretical construct.

In the next decade this could change. An intriguing outcome of theoretical developments since 1995 is the recognition that strings and the extra dimensions might be significantly larger than previously thought. Rather than being 10^{-33} cm, studies with the more refined M-theory framework have established that strings could be larger by many orders of magnitude. If so, the next generation of particle accelerators (such as the Large Hadron Collider at CERN) may have enough energy to probe the physical properties of strings directly, providing the long-sought experimental confirmation of the theory.

The experiments at CERN will also search for evidence of supersymmetry, a mathematical property discovered within string theory that requires every known particle species to have a partner particle species, called superpartners. (This property accounts for string theory often being referred to as superstring theory.) As yet, no superpartner particles have been detected, but researchers believe this may be due to their weight—they are heavier than their known counterparts and require a machine at least as powerful as the Large Hadron Collider to produce them. If the superpartner particles are found, string theory still will not be proved correct, because more conventional point-particle theories have also successfully incorporated supersymmetry into their mathematical structure. However, the discovery of supersymmetry would confirm an essential element of string theory and give circumstantial evidence that this approach to unification is on the right track.

Even if these accelerator-based tests are inconclusive, there is another way that string theory may one day be tested. Through its impact on the earliest, most extreme moments of the universe, the physics of string theory may have left faint cosmological signatures—for example, in the form of gravitational waves or a particular pattern of temperature variations in the cosmic microwave background radiation—that may be observable by the next generation of precision satellite-borne telescopes and detectors. It would be a fitting conclusion to Einstein's quest for unification if a theory of the smallest microscopic component of matter were confirmed through observations of the largest astronomical realms of the cosmos.

CHAPTER 3

PARTICLE ACCELERATORS

Aparticle accelerator is any device that produces a beam of fast-moving, electrically charged atomic or subatomic particles. Physicists use accelerators in fundamental research on the structure of nuclei, the nature of nuclear forces, and the properties of nuclei not found in nature, as in the transuranium elements and other unstable elements. Accelerators are also used for radioisotope production, industrial radiography, radiation therapy, sterilization of biological materials, and a certain form of radiocarbon dating. The largest accelerators are used in research on the fundamental interactions of the elementary subatomic particles.

PRINCIPLES OF PARTICLE ACCELERATION

Particle accelerators exist in many shapes and sizes (even the ubiquitous television picture tube is in principle a particle accelerator), but the smallest accelerators share common elements with the larger devices. First, all accelerators must have a source that generates electrically charged particles—electrons in the case of the television tube and electrons, protons, and their antiparticles in the case of larger accelerators. All accelerators must have electric fields to accelerate the particles, and they must have magnetic fields to control the paths of the particles. Also, the particles must travel through a good vacuum—that is, in a container with as little residual air as possible, as in a television tube. Finally, all accelerators must have some means of detecting, counting, and measuring the particles after they have been accelerated through the vacuum.

GENERATING PARTICLES

Electrons and protons, the particles most commonly used in accelerators, are found in all materials, but for an accelerator the appropriate particles must be separated out. Electrons are usually produced in exactly the same way as in a television picture tube, in a device known as an electron "gun." The gun contains a cathode (negative electrode) in a vacuum, which is heated so that electrons break away from the atoms in the cathode material. The emitted electrons, which are negatively charged, are attracted toward an anode (positive electrode), where they pass through a hole. The gun itself is in effect a simple accelerator, because the electrons move through an electric field, as described later in the chapter. The voltage between the cathode and the anode in an electron gun is typically 50,000–150,000 volts, or 50–150 kilovolts (kV).

As with electrons, there are protons in all materials, but only the nuclei of hydrogen atoms consist of single protons, so hydrogen gas is the source of particles for proton accelerators. In this case the gas is ionized— the electrons and protons are separated in an electric field—and the protons escape through a hole. In large high-energy particle accelerators, protons are often produced initially in the form of negative hydrogen ions. These are hydrogen atoms with an extra electron, which are also formed when the gas, originally in the form of molecules of two atoms, is ionized. Negative hydrogen ions prove easier to handle in the initial stages of large accelerators. They are later passed through thin foils to strip off the electrons before the protons move to the final stage of acceleration.

ACCELERATING PARTICLES

The key feature of any particle accelerator is the accelerating electric field. The simplest example is a uniform static field between positive and negative electric potentials (voltages), much like the field that exists between the terminals of an electric battery. In such a field an electron, bearing a negative charge, feels a force that directs it toward the positive potential (akin to the positive terminal of the battery). This force accelerates the electron, and if there is nothing to impede the electron, its velocity and its energy will increase. Electrons moving toward a positive potential along a wire or even in air will collide with atoms and lose energy, but if the electrons pass through a vacuum, they will accelerate as they move toward the positive potential.

The difference in electric potential between the position where the electron begins moving through the field and the place where it leaves the field determines the energy that the electron acquires. The energy an electron gains in traveling through a potential difference of 1 volt is known as 1 electron volt (eV). This is a tiny amount of energy, equivalent to 1.6×10^{-19} joule. A flying mosquito has about a trillion times this energy. However, in a television tube, electrons are accelerated through more than 10,000 volts, giving them energies above 10,000 eV, or 10 kiloelectron volts (keV). Many particle accelerators reach much higher energies, measured in megaelectron volts (MeV, or million eV), gigaelectron volts (GeV, or billion eV), or teraelectron volts (TeV, or trillion eV).

Some of the earliest designs for particle accelerators, such as the voltage multiplier and the Van de Graaff generator, used constant electric fields created by potentials up to a million volts. It is not easy to work with such high voltages, however. A more-practical alternative is to make repeated use of weaker electric fields set up by lower voltages. This is the principle involved in two common categories of modern particle accelerators—linear accelerators (or linacs) and cyclic accelerators (principally the cyclotron and the synchrotron). In a linear accelerator the particles pass once through a sequence of accelerating fields, whereas in a cyclic machine they are guided on a circular path many times through the same relatively small electric fields. In both cases the final energy of the particles depends on the cumulative effect of the fields, so that many small "pushes" add together to give the combined effect of one big "push."

The repetitive structure of a linear accelerator naturally suggests the use of alternating rather than constant voltages to create the electric fields. A positively charged particle accelerated toward a negative potential, for example, will receive a renewed push if the potential becomes positive as the particle passes by. In practice the voltages must change quite rapidly. For example, at an energy of 1 MeV a proton is already traveling at very high speeds—46 percent of the speed of light—so that it covers a distance of about 1.4 metres (4.6 feet) in 0.01 microsecond. (One microsecond is a millionth of a second.) This implies that in a repeated structure several metres long, the electric fields must alternate—that is, change direction—at a frequency of at least 100 million cycles per second, or 100 megahertz (MHz). Both linear and cyclic accelerators generally accelerate particles by using the alternating electric fields present in electromagnetic waves, typically at frequencies from 100 to 3,000 MHz—that is, ranging from radiowaves to microwaves.

An electromagnetic wave is in effect a combination of oscillating electric and magnetic fields vibrating at right angles to each other. The key with a particle accelerator is to set up the wave so that, when the particles arrive, the electric field is in the direction needed to accelerate the particles. This can be done with a standing wave—a combination of waves moving in opposite directions in an enclosed space, rather like sound waves vibrating in an organ pipe. Alternatively, for extremely fast-moving electrons, which travel very close to the speed of light (in other words, close to the speed of the wave itself), a traveling wave can be used for acceleration.

An important effect that comes into play in acceleration in an alternating electric field is that of "phase stability." In one cycle of its oscillation, an alternating field passes from zero through a maximum value to zero again and then falls to a minimum before rising back to zero. This means that the field passes twice through the value appropriate for acceleration—for example, during the rise and fall through the maximum. If a particle whose velocity is increasing arrives too soon as the field rises, it will not experience as high a field as it should and so will not receive as big a push. However, when it reaches the next region of accelerating fields, it will arrive late and so will receive a higher field—in other words, too big a push. The net effect will be phase stability—that is, the particle will be kept in phase with the field in each accelerating region. Another effect will be a grouping of the particles in time, so that they will form a train of bunches rather than a continuous beam of particles.

GUIDING PARTICLES

Magnetic fields also play an important role in particle accelerators, as they can change the direction of charged particles. This means that they can be used to "bend" particle beams around a circular path so that they pass repeatedly through the same accelerating regions. In the simplest case a charged particle moving in a direction at right angles to the direction of a uniform magnetic field feels a force at right angles both to the particle's direction and to the field. The effect of this force is to make the particle move on a circular path, perpendicular to the field, until it leaves the region of magnetic force or another force acts upon it. This effect comes into play in cyclic accelerators such as cyclotrons and synchrotrons. In the cyclotron a large magnet is used to provide a constant field in which the particles spiral outward as they are fed energy and thereby accelerate on each circuit. In a synchrotron, by contrast, the particles move around a ring of constant radius, while the field generated by electromagnets around the ring is increased as the particles accelerate. The magnets with this "bending" function are dipoles—magnets with two poles, north and south, built with a C-shaped profile so that the particle beam can pass between the two poles.

A second important function of electromagnets in particle accelerators is to focus the particle beams in order to keep them as narrow and intense as possible. The simplest form of focusing magnet is a quadrupole, a magnet built with four poles (two norths and two souths) arranged opposite each other. This arrangement pushes particles toward the centre in one direction but allows them to spread in the perpendicular direction. A quadrupole designed to focus a beam horizontally, therefore, will let the beam go out of focus vertically. In order to provide proper focusing, quadrupole magnets must be used in pairs, each member arranged to have the opposite effect. More complex magnets with larger numbers of poles—sextupoles and octupoles—are also used for more sophisticated focusing.

As the energy of the circulating particles increases, the strength of the magnetic field guiding them is increased, which thus keeps the particles on the same path. A "pulse" of particles is injected into the ring and accelerated to the desired energy before it is extracted and delivered to experiments. Extraction is usually achieved by "kicker" magnets, electromagnets that switch on just long enough to "kick" the particles out of the synchrotron ring and along a beam line. The fields in the dipole magnets are then ramped down, and the machine is ready to receive its next pulse of particles.

COLLIDING PARTICLES

Most of the particle accelerators used in medicine and industry produce a beam of particles for a specific purpose—for example, for radiation therapy or ion implantation. This means that the particles are used once and then discarded. For many years the same was true for accelerators used in particle physics research. However, in the 1970s rings were developed in which two beams of particles circulate in opposite directions and collide on each circuit of the machine. A major advantage of such machines is that when two beams collide head-on, the energy of the particles goes directly into the energy of the interactions between them. This contrasts with what happens when an energetic beam collides with material at rest: in this case much of the energy is lost in setting the target material in motion, in accord with the principle of conservation of momentum.

Some colliding-beam machines have been built with two rings that cross at two or more positions, with beams of the same kind circulating in opposite directions. More common yet have been particle-antiparticle colliders. An antiparticle has opposite electric charge to its related particle. For example, an antielectron (or positron) has positive charge, while the electron has negative charge. This means that an electric field that accelerates an electron will decelerate a positron moving in the same direction as the electron. But if the positron is traveling through the field in the opposite direction, it will feel an opposite force and will be accelerated. Similarly, an electron moving though a magnetic field will be bent in one direction—left, say—while a positron moving the same way will be bent in the opposite direction—to the right. If, however, the positron moves through the magnetic field in the opposite direction to the electron, its path will still bend to the right, but along the same curve taken by the leftward-bending electron. Taken together, these effects mean that an antielectron can travel around a synchrotron ring guided by the same magnets and accelerated by the same electric fields that affect an electron traveling the opposite way. Many of the highest-energy colliding-beam machines have been particle-antiparticle colliders, as only one accelerator ring is needed.

As was pointed out earlier, the beam in a synchrotron is not a continuous stream of particles but is clustered into "bunches." A bunch may be a few centimetres long and a tenth of a millimetre across, and it may contain about 10^{12} particles—the actual numbers depending on the specific machine. However, this is not especially dense. Normal matter of similar dimensions contains about 10^{23} atoms. So when particle beams—or, more accurately, particle bunches—cross in a colliding-beam machine, there is only a small chance that two particles will interact. In practice the bunches can continue around the ring and intersect again. To enable this repeated beam crossing, the vacuum in the rings of colliding-beam machines must be particularly good so that the particles can circulate for many hours without being lost through collisions with residual air molecules. The rings are therefore also referred to as storage rings, as the particle beams are in effect stored within them for several hours.

DETECTING PARTICLES

Most uses of the beams from particle accelerators require some way of detecting what happens when the particles strike a target or another particle beam traveling in the opposite direction. In a television picture tube, the electrons shot from the electron gun strike special phosphors on the inside surface of the screen, and these emit light, which thereby re-creates the televised images. With particle accelerators similarly specialized detectors respond to scattered particles, but these detectors are usually designed to create electrical signals that can be transformed into computer data and analyzed by computer programs. Only electrically charged particles create electrical signals as they move through a material—for example, by exciting or ionizing the atoms—and can be detected directly. Neutral particles, such as neutrons or photons, must be detected indirectly through the behaviour of charged particles that they themselves set in motion.

There are a great variety of particle detectors, many of which are most useful in specific circumstances. Some, such as the familiar Geiger counter, simply count particles, whereas others are used, for example, to record the tracks of charged particles or to measure the velocity of a particle or the amount of energy it carries. Modern detectors vary in size and technology from small charge-coupled devices (CCDs) to large gas-filled chambers threaded with wires that sense the ionized trails created by charged particles.

HISTORY

Most of the development of particle accelerators has been motivated by research into the properties of atomic nuclei and subatomic particles. Starting with British physicist Ernest Rutherford's discovery in 1919 of a reaction between a nitrogen nucleus and an alpha particle, all research in nuclear physics until 1932 was performed with alpha particles released by the decay of naturally radioactive elements. Natural alpha particles have kinetic energies as high as 8 MeV, but Rutherford believed that, in order to observe the disintegration of heavier nuclei by alpha particles, it would be necessary to accelerate alpha particle ions artificially to even higher energies. At that time there seemed little hope of generating laboratory voltages sufficient to accelerate ions to the desired energies. However, a calculation made in 1928 by George Gamow (then at the University of Göttingen, Ger.) indicated that considerably less-energetic ions could be useful, and this stimulated attempts to build an accelerator that could provide a beam of particles suitable for nuclear research.

Other developments of that period demonstrated principles still employed in the design of particle accelerators. The first successful experiments with artificially accelerated ions were performed in England at the University of Cambridge by John Douglas Cockcroft and E.T.S. Walton in 1932. Using a voltage multiplier, they accelerated protons to energies as high as 710 keV and showed that these react with the lithium nucleus to produce two energetic alpha particles. By 1931, at Princeton University in New Jersey, Robert J. Van de Graaff had constructed the first belt-charged electrostatic high-voltage generator. Cockcroft-Walton-type voltage multipliers and Van de Graaff generators are still employed as power sources for accelerators.

The principle of the linear resonance accelerator was demonstrated by Rolf Wideröe in 1928. At the Rhenish-Westphalian Technical University in Aachen, Ger., Wideröe used alternating high voltage to accelerate ions of sodium and potassium to energies twice as high as those imparted by one application of the peak voltage. In 1931 in the United States, Ernest O. Lawrence and his assistant David H. Sloan, at the University of California, Berkeley, employed high-frequency fields to accelerate mercury ions to more than 1.2 MeV. This work augmented Wideröe's achievement in accelerating heavy ions, but the ion beams were not useful in nuclear research.

The magnetic resonance accelerator, or cyclotron, was conceived by Lawrence as a modification of Wideröe's linear resonance accelerator. Lawrence's student M.S. Livingston demonstrated the principle of the cyclotron in 1931, producing 80-keV ions. In 1932 Lawrence and Livingston announced the acceleration of protons to more than 1 MeV. Later in the 1930s, cyclotron energies reached about 25 MeV and Van de Graaff generators about 4 MeV. In 1940 Donald W. Kerst, applying the results of careful orbit calculations to the design of magnets, constructed the first betatron, a magnetic-induction accelerator of electrons, at the University of Illinois.

Following World War II there was a rapid advance in the science of accelerating particles to high energies. Progress was initiated by Edwin Mattison McMillan at Berkeley and by Vladimir Iosifovich Veksler at Moscow. In 1945 both men independently described the principle

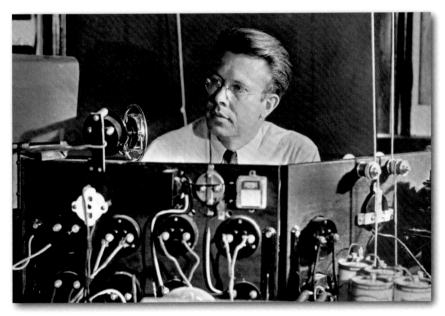

Ernest Orlando Lawrence at the controls of a cyclotron. University of California, Lawrence Berkeley Lab

of phase stability. This concept suggested a means of maintaining stable particle orbits in the cyclic accelerator and thus removed an apparent limitation on the energy of resonance accelerators for protons and made possible the construction of magnetic resonance accelerators (called synchrotrons) for electrons. Phase focusing, the implementation of the principle of phase stability, was promptly demonstrated by the construction of a small synchrocyclotron at the University of California and an electron synchrotron in England. The first proton linear resonance accelerator was constructed soon thereafter. The large proton synchrotrons that have been built since then all depend on this principle.

In 1947 William W. Hansen, at Stanford University in California, constructed the first traveling-wave linear accelerator of electrons, exploiting microwave technology that had been developed for radar during World War II.

The progress in research made possible by raising the energies of protons led to the building of successively larger accelerators. The trend was ended only by the cost of fabricating the huge magnet rings required—the largest weighs approximately 40,000 tons. A means of increasing the energy without increasing the scale of the machines was provided by a demonstration in 1952 by Livingston, Ernest D. Courant, and H.S. Snyder of the technique of alternating-gradient focusing (sometimes called strong focusing). Synchrotrons incorporating this principle needed magnets only $\frac{1}{100}$ the size that would be required otherwise. All recently constructed synchrotrons make use of alternating-gradient focusing.

In 1956 Kerst realized that, if two sets of particles could be maintained in intersecting orbits, it should be possible to observe interactions in which one particle collided with another moving in the opposite direction. Application of this idea requires the accumulation of accelerated particles in loops called storage rings. The highest reaction energies now obtainable have been produced by the use of this technique.

CONSTANT-VOLTAGE ACCELERATORS

The simplest type of particle accelerator is constructed by mounting a particle source on one end of an insulated, evacuated tube and creating a high voltage between the ends, with the polarity such that the particles are impelled from the source toward the far end of the tube. Such an accelerator is necessarily linear, and the electrostatic field can be applied to a given particle only once (unless, as in the tandem accelerator described below, the charge of the particle undergoes a change in sign). The simplicity of concept becomes complex in execution when the electric potential exceeds one million volts (1 megavolt, or 1 MV). These high voltages produce corona discharges and lightninglike sparks outside the accelerator, which dissipate the potential needed to accelerate the particles. Even more difficult to control are sparks within the equipment and, in positive-ion accelerators, unwanted secondary beams produced when the accelerated ions strike the end of the tube.

VOLTAGE MULTIPLIERS (CASCADE GENERATORS)

The source of the high voltage for Cockcroft and Walton's pioneering experiments was a four-stage voltage multiplier assembled from four large rectifiers and high-voltage capacitors. Their circuit in effect combined four rectifier-type direct-voltage power supplies in series. The alternating voltage supplied by a high-voltage transformer was transmitted to the higher stages through an array of capacitors. A second group of capacitors kept the direct voltage constant. The final direct voltage would have been four times the peak voltage available from the transformer (200,000 volts) if corona discharge had not drained away considerable power. Nevertheless, the apparatus did accelerate protons to energies of 710 keV, sufficient to bring about the hoped-for result, a reaction with lithium nuclei. This achievement, the first nuclear reaction effected by artificially accelerated particles, was recognized by the award of the Nobel Prize for Physics in 1951.

Cockcroft and Walton's system for building up high direct voltages can be extended to multiplication factors many times that originally demonstrated. Commercially available accelerators that reach 4 MeV are based on this circuitry.

Van de Graaff Generators

In Van de Graaff generators, electric charge is transported to the high-voltage terminal on a rapidly moving belt of insulating material driven by a pulley mounted on the grounded end of the structure. A second pulley is enclosed within a large, spherical high-voltage terminal. The belt is charged by a comb of sharp needles with the points close to the belt a short distance from the place at which it moves clear of the grounded pulley. The comb is connected to a power supply that raises its potential to a few tens of kilovolts. The gas near the needle points is ionized by the intense electric field, and in the resulting corona discharge the ions are driven to the surface of the belt. The motion of the belt carries the charge into the high-voltage terminal and transfers it to another comb of needles, from which it passes to the outer surface of the terminal. A carefully designed Van de Graaff generator insulated by pressurized gas can be charged to a potential of about 20 megavolts. An ion source within the terminal then produces positive particles that are accelerated as they move downward to ground potential through an evacuated tube.

In most constant-voltage accelerators, Van de Graaff generators are the source of high voltage, and most of the electrostatic proton accelerators still in use are two-stage tandem accelerators. These devices provide a beam with twice the energy that could be achieved by one application of the high voltage. For the first stage of a tandem accelerator, an ion source yields a beam of protons, which are accelerated to a low energy by an auxiliary high-voltage supply. This beam passes through a region containing a gas at low pressure, where some of

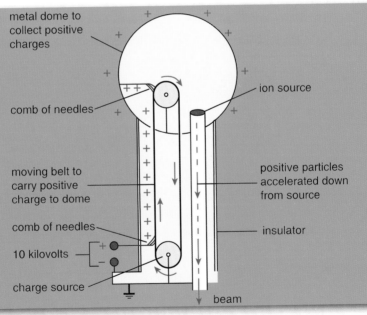

Schematic diagram of a Van de Graaff high-voltage electrostatic generator. High voltages introduced at the charge source are transferred by a moving belt to the spherical dome, where the accumulated positive charge propels a beam of positively charged subatomic particles the length of an accelerating tube. First built in the 1930s, Van de Graaff generators are still used in particle acceleration. Copyright Encyclopædia Britannica; rendering for this edition by Rosen Educational Services

the protons are converted to negative hydrogen ions by the addition of two electrons. As the mixture of charged particles moves through a magnetic field, those with positive charge are deflected away. Those with negative charge are deflected into the accelerator tube, and the beam of negative ions is then accelerated toward a positive high-voltage terminal. In this terminal the particles pass through a thin carbon foil that strips off the two electrons, changing many of the negative ions back into positive ions (protons). These, now repelled by the positive terminal, are further accelerated through the second part of the tube. At the output end of the accelerator, the protons are magnetically separated, as before, from other particles in the beam and directed to the target. In three- or four-stage tandem accelerators, two Van de Graaff generators are combined with the necessary additional provisions for changing the charge of the ions.

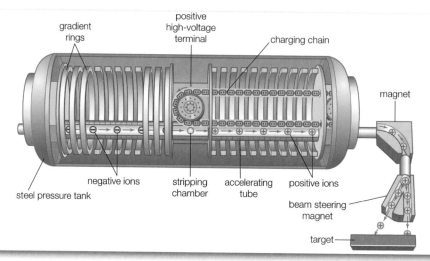

Two-stage tandem particle accelerator. A beam of negative ions enters from the top and is accelerated toward the positive terminal at the centre. There it passes through carbon foil in a stripping chamber, where many of the negative ions lose electrons and emerge as positive ions. The beam is then accelerated away from the positive terminal, and the positive ions are separated by magnets and steered toward the target. Encyclopædia Britannica, Inc.

Van de Graaff and Cockcroft-Walton generators are also used for accelerating electrons. The rates at which charge is transported in electron beams correspond to currents of several milliamperes; the beams deliver energy at rates best expressed in terms of kilowatts. These intense beams are used for sterilization, industrial radiography, cancer therapy, and processing of plastics.

BETATRONS

A betatron is a type of accelerator that is useful only for electrons, which are sometimes called beta particles—hence the name. The electrons in a betatron move in a circle under the influence of a magnetic field that increases in strength as the energy of the electrons is increased. The magnet that produces the field on the electron orbit also produces a field in the interior of the orbit. The increase in the strength of this field with time produces an electric field that accelerates the electrons. If the average magnetic field inside the orbit is always twice as strong as the magnetic field on the orbit, the radius of the orbit remains constant, so that the acceleration chamber can be made in the shape of a torus, or doughnut. The poles of the magnet are tapered to cause the field near the orbit to weaken with increasing radius. This focuses the beam by causing any particle that strays from the orbit to be subjected to forces that restore it toward its proper path. The theory of this focusing was first worked out for the betatron. By analogy, the oscillations of particles about their equilibrium orbits in all cyclic accelerators are called betatron oscillations.

Just after the sinusoidally varying strength of the magnetic field has passed through zero and starts increasing in the direction proper to guide the electrons in their circular orbit, a burst of electrons is sent into the doughnut, where—in a 20-MeV betatron—they gain about 100 eV per revolution and traverse the orbit about 200,000 times during the acceleration. The acceleration lasts for one-quarter of the magnet cycle until the magnetic field has reached its greatest strength, whereupon the orbit is caused to shrink, deflecting the electrons onto a target—for example, to produce a beam of intense X-rays.

The practical limit on the energy imparted by a betatron is set by the emission of electromagnetic energy from electrons moving in curved paths. The intensity of this radiation, commonly called synchrotron radiation, rises rapidly as the speed of the electrons increases. The largest betatron accelerates electrons to 300 MeV, sufficient to produce pi-mesons in its target. The energy loss by its electrons through radiation (a few percent) is compensated by changing the relation between the field on the orbit and the average field inside the orbit. At higher energies this compensation would not be feasible.

Betatrons are now commercially manufactured, principally for use as sources of X-rays for industrial radiography and for radiation therapy in medicine. X-ray beams are produced when an electron beam is directed onto a target material with a heavy atomic nucleus, such as platinum.

CYCLOTRONS

The magnetic resonance accelerator, or cyclotron, was the first cyclic accelerator and the first resonance accelerator that produced particles energetic enough to be useful for nuclear research. For many years the highest particle energies were those imparted by cyclotrons modeled upon Lawrence's archetype. In these devices, commonly called classical cyclotrons, the accelerating electric field oscillates at a fixed frequency, and the guiding magnetic field has a fixed intensity.

CLASSICAL CYCLOTRONS

The key to the operation of a cyclotron is the fact that the orbits of ions in a uniform magnetic field are isochronous. That is, the time taken by a particle of a given mass to make one complete circuit is the same at any speed or energy as long as the speed is much less than that of light. (As the speed of a particle approaches that of light, its mass increases as predicted by the theory of relativity.) This isochronicity makes it possible for a high voltage, reversing in polarity at a constant frequency, to accelerate a particle many times. An ion source is located at the centre of an evacuated chamber that has the shape of a short cylinder, like a pillbox, between the poles of an electromagnet that creates a uniform field perpendicular to the flat faces. The accelerating voltage is applied by electrodes, called dees from their shape: each is a D-shaped half of a pillbox. The source of the voltage is an oscillator—similar to a radio transmitter—that operates at a frequency equal to the frequency of revolution of the particles in the magnetic field. The electric fields caused by this accelerating voltage are concentrated in the gap between the dees. There is no electric field inside the dees. The path of the particle inside the dees is therefore circular. Each time the particle crosses the gap between the dees, it is accelerated, because in the time between these crossings the direction of the field reverses. The path of the particle is thus a spiral-like series of semicircles of continually increasing radius.

Some means of focusing is required. Otherwise, a particle that starts out in a direction making a small angle with the orbital plane will spiral into the dees and be lost. While the energy of the particle is still low, this focusing is supplied by the accelerating electric fields. After the particle has gained significant energy, focusing is a

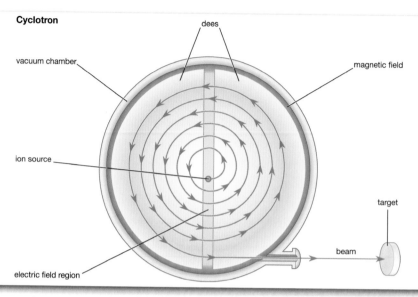

Cyclotron

dees

vacuum chamber

magnetic field

ion source

target

beam

electric field region

Plan view of a classical cyclotron. Subatomic particles introduced into the middle of the cyclotron are induced by a magnetic field to follow a spiraling circular path through two hollow semicircular structures called dees. Each time they cross the gap between the dees, the particles are accelerated by an electric field until they emerge in a coherent beam. Developed in the 1930s, classical cyclotrons are still used to produce radioactive isotopes for medical diagnosis. Encyclopædia Britannica, Inc.

consequence of a slight weakening of the magnetic field toward the peripheries of the dees, as in the betatron.

The energy gained by a particle in a classical cyclotron is limited by the relativistic increase in the mass of the particle, a phenomenon that causes the orbital frequency to decrease and the particles to get out of phase with the alternating voltage. This effect can be reduced by applying higher accelerating voltages to shorten the overall acceleration time. The highest energy imparted to protons in a classical cyclotron is less than 25 MeV, and this achievement requires the imposition of hundreds of kilovolts to the dees. The beam current in a classical cyclotron operated at high voltages can be as high as five milliamperes. Intensities of this magnitude are very useful in the synthesis of radioisotopes.

SYNCHROCYCLOTRONS

Cyclotrons in which the frequency of the accelerating voltage is changed as the particles are accelerated are called synchrocyclotrons, frequency-modulated (FM) cyclotrons, or phasotrons. Because of the modulation, the particles do not get out of phase with the accelerating voltage, so that the relativistic mass increase does not impose a limit on the energy. Moreover, the magnetic focusing can be made stronger, so that the magnetic field need not be so precisely shaped.

Because of the phenomenon of phase stability, it is unnecessary to program the frequency of the accelerating voltage precisely to follow the decreasing frequency of revolution of the particles as they are accelerated. To see how phase stability affects the operation of a cyclotron, consider a particle moving in an orbit. Let the frequency of the accelerating voltage match the orbital frequency of this particle. If the particle crosses the accelerating gap at the time the accelerating voltage is zero, its energy and orbital radius will remain unchanged. It is said to be in equilibrium. There are two such times during each cycle of the accelerating voltage. Only one of these (that at which the voltage is falling, rather than rising, through zero) corresponds to stable equilibrium. If a particle should arrive a short time before the voltage has fallen to zero, it is accelerated. Its speed therefore increases, but the radius of its orbit increases by an even larger proportion, so that the particle will take longer to reach the gap again and will next cross it at a time closer to that at which it would receive no acceleration. If, however, the particle reaches the gap a short time after the voltage has fallen through zero, its speed is diminished, and the radius of its orbit is diminished even more, so that it takes less time to reach the gap again, arriving—like the other particle—at a time closer to that at which it receives no acceleration. This phenomenon, by which the trajectories of errant particles are continually corrected, confers stability on the entire beam and makes it possible to accelerate the particles uniformly, by modulating the frequency, without dispersing them. The small periodic variations of the particles about the equilibrium values of phase and energy are called synchrotron oscillations.

In the operation of a synchrocyclotron, particles are accelerated from the ion source when the frequency of the accelerating voltage is equal to the orbital frequency of the particles in the central field. As the frequency of the voltage falls, the particles, on the average, encounter an accelerating field. They oscillate in phase but around a value that corresponds to the average acceleration. The particles reach the maximum energy in bunches, one for each time the accelerating frequency goes through its program. The intensity of the beam is a few microamperes, much lower than that of a classical cyclotron.

Large synchrocyclotrons have been constructed in many countries. They are used primarily for research with secondary beams of pi-mesons. The practical upper limit of the energy of a synchrocyclotron, set by the cost of the huge magnets required, is about 1 GeV.

SECTOR-FOCUSED CYCLOTRONS

The sector-focused cyclotron is another modification of the classical cyclotron that also evades relativistic constraint on its maximum energy. Its advantage over the synchrocyclotron is that the beam is not pulsed and is more intense. The frequency of the accelerating voltage is constant, and the orbital frequency of the particles is kept constant as they are accelerated by causing the average magnetic field on the orbit to increase with orbit radius. This ordinarily would cause the beam to spread out in the direction of the magnetic field, but in sector-focused cyclotrons the magnetic field varies with the angular position as well as with the radius. This produces the equivalent of alternating-gradient focusing. This principle was discovered in 1938 by Llewellyn H. Thomas, then at Ohio State University, but was not applied until the alternating-gradient synchrotron was invented in 1952. Several of these devices, sometimes called azimuthally varying field (AVF) cyclotrons, have been built for use in nuclear and medical research. The world's largest cyclotron, at the TRIUMF laboratory in Vancouver, B.C., Can., is a sector-focused machine. Its magnet, which weighs 4,000 metric tons and is 18 metres (59 feet) in diameter, is divided into six equal sectors arranged like a pinwheel. Its maximum energy is 520 MeV, and it is used mainly for research in subatomic particle physics.

LINEAR RESONANCE ACCELERATORS

The technology required for designing a useful linear resonance accelerator was developed after 1940. These accelerators require very powerful sources of radio-frequency accelerating voltage. Further, a practical linear accelerator for heavy particles, such as protons, must make use of the principle of phase stability.

Linear accelerators fall into two distinct types: standing-wave linear accelerators (used for heavy particles) and traveling-wave linear accelerators (used to accelerate electrons). The reason for the difference is that, after electrons have been accelerated to a few megaelectron volts in the first few metres of a typical accelerator, they have speeds very close to that of light. Therefore, if the accelerating wave also moves at the speed of light, the particles do not get out of phase, as their speeds do not change. Protons, however, must reach much higher energies before their speeds can be taken as constant, so the accelerator design must allow for the prolonged increase in speed.

LINEAR ELECTRON ACCELERATORS

The force that acts on electrons in a traveling-wave accelerator is provided by an electromagnetic field with a frequency near 3,000 MHz (1 MHz = 1,000,000 Hertz, or 1,000,000 cycles per second)—a microwave. The acceleration chamber is an evacuated cylindrical pipe that serves as a waveguide for the accelerating field. The phase velocity of an electromagnetic wave in a cylindrical pipe is greater than the velocity of light in free space, so the wave must be slowed down by the insertion of metal irises a few centimetres apart in the pipe. In the intense field the electrons gain about 2 MeV every 30 centimetres (12 inches) or so. The microwaves are produced by large klystrons (high-frequency vacuum-tube amplifiers) with power outputs of 20–30 megawatts. Because sources of radio-frequency power of this magnitude must be operated intermittently (they will not survive continuous service), the beams from these accelerators are delivered in short bursts.

Pulses of electrons are injected at energies of a few hundred kiloelectron volts (that is, speeds about half that

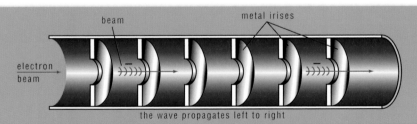

Acceleration chamber of a linear electron accelerator. The chamber, essentially a sealed pipe, acts as a waveguide for the accelerating electromagnetic wave. The metal irises decrease the phase velocity of the wave, which accelerates pulses of electrons almost to the speed of light. Copyright Encyclopædia Britannica; rendering for this edition by Rosen Educational Services of light). The accelerator is so designed that, during the first part of the acceleration, the electrons are caused to gather into bunches, which then are accelerated nearly to the speed of light. Subsequently, the electrons move with the crest of the electromagnetic wave.

Linear electron accelerators are manufactured commercially. They are used for radiography, for cancer treatment, and as injectors for electron synchrotrons.

The 3.2-km (2-mile) linear electron accelerator at the Stanford Linear Accelerator Center (SLAC) in California is the source of extremely energetic beams of electrons and positrons, up to a maximum of 50 GeV. The positrons are produced as secondary particles when the electron beam is allowed to strike a target one-third of the distance along the accelerator, and they are later fed back into the machine, alternately with electrons, for acceleration along

The Stanford Linear Accelerator Center, Menlo Park, Calif., has a 3.2-km (2-mile) linear electron accelerator, the longest linear accelerator in the world. Stanford Linear Accelerator Center

its full length. In the Stanford Linear Collider (SLC), which operated from 1989 to 1998, the electrons and positrons were directed into two separate arcs of magnets at the far end of the accelerator. The arcs formed a loop to bring the two beams into head-on collision at a total energy of about 100 GeV.

Linear electron accelerators constructed of superconducting materials have been developed. Such structures dissipate far less energy than conventional metal structures, allowing a continuous electron beam, rather than a pulsed beam, to be accelerated. This principle is being exploited to good effect at the Continuous Electron Beam Accelerator Facility (CEBAF) in Newport News, Va. This consists of two 250-metre (820-foot) linear accelerators joined at each end by semicircular arcs to form an oval "racetrack." Electrons are injected at 45 MeV and can be accelerated to energies of 4 GeV or more, the highest energies being reached after the beams have completed five circuits of the machine.

LINEAR PROTON ACCELERATORS

The design principle applied in linear accelerators for protons was originated by Luis Alvarez at Berkeley in 1946. It is based on the formation of standing electromagnetic waves in a long cylindrical metal tank or cavity. In the design that has been adopted, the electric field is parallel to the axis of the tank. Most of these accelerators operate at frequencies of about 200 MHz—lower than the frequencies employed in linear electron accelerators, owing to the lower velocity of the heavier protons.

During the time required for a proton to traverse one of these tanks, the accelerating electric fields undergo many reversals of direction. In Alvarez's design the decelerating effect of the field during the intervals when it opposes the motion of the particles is prevented by installing on the

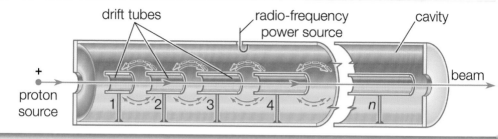

Schematic diagram of a linear proton resonance accelerator. The accelerator is a large-diameter tube within which an electric field oscillates at a high radio frequency. Within the accelerator tube are smaller diameter metallic drift tubes, which are carefully sized and spaced to shield the protons from decelerating oscillations of the electric field. In the spaces between the drift tubes, the electric field is oriented properly to accelerate the protons in their direction of travel. Encyclopædia Britannica, Inc.

axis of the tank a number of "drift tubes." The electric field is zero inside the drift tubes, and, if their lengths are properly chosen, the protons cross the gap between adjacent drift tubes when the direction of the field produces acceleration and are shielded by the drift tubes when the field in the tank would decelerate them. The lengths of the drift tubes are proportional to the speeds of the particles that pass through them.

It would appear that any error in the magnitude of the accelerating voltages would cause the particles to lose the synchronism with the fields needed for proper operation of the device, but the principle of phase stability reduces to a manageable magnitude the need for precision in construction. It also makes possible an intense beam because protons can be accelerated in a stable manner even if they do not cross the gaps at exactly the intended times. The principle is the same as that of a synchrotron, except that the gap-crossing time for stable phase oscillations coincides with the rise, rather than the fall, of the voltage wave. If a proton arrives at the accelerating gap late, it receives a larger-than-normal increment of energy, enabling it to "catch up."

An exceptionally large amount of radio-frequency power is required for producing the accelerating voltages. This makes it necessary for linear proton accelerators to be operated in a pulsed mode. They are supplied with protons accelerated to about 750 keV by a Cockcroft-Walton generator. The entering beam passes through an accelerating radio-frequency cavity a short distance upbeam from the main linear accelerator, so that, as the particles pass through the first drift tubes, they are already bunched.

As the particle energy increases in the Alvarez design, the drift tubes become longer, and an increasing proportion of the energy stored in the system is not used for acceleration. A more efficient design, developed at the Los Alamos National Laboratory in New Mexico, is the side-coupled-cavity structure. In this design walls divide the long Alvarez tank into individual cavities that are linked by relatively short drift tubes. Smaller cavities along one side feed radio-frequency power to pairs of adjacent accelerating cavities in such a way that an alternating electric field is set up along the axis of the overall cylindrical structure. Particles traveling along the axis pass from one cell to the next just as the alternating electric field reverses direction, so they always experience an accelerating field. As the velocity of the particles increases, the lengths of the cavities must also increase along the accelerator.

The highest-energy proton linear accelerator is at the Los Alamos National Laboratory. The protons are accelerated to 100 MeV in Alvarez-type tanks and then to 800 MeV in a standing-wave linear accelerator of the side-coupled-cavity type operated at a frequency of 805 MHz. The accelerator, 785 metres (2,500 feet) long, produces a beam carrying a current in excess of one milliampere, which delivers a power of more than 800 kilowatts. It was built in the late 1960s to provide beams for nuclear research, in particular intense secondary beams of pi-mesons, but it has since become more important as a source of protons to generate neutron beams. Since 1995 it has formed part of the Los Alamos Neutron Science Center (LANSCE), dedicated to research with neutrons.

The intense pulses of protons produced by linear accelerators make them useful injectors for proton synchrotrons. The highest-energy injector of this kind is at the Fermi National Accelerator Laboratory (Fermilab) in Batavia, Ill. The 150-metre- (500-foot-) long machine consists of five Alvarez-type tanks followed by a side-coupled-cavity linear accelerator that accelerates to a final energy of 400 MeV.

SYNCHROTRONS

As the particles in a synchrotron are accelerated, the strength of the magnetic field is increased to keep the radius of the orbit approximately constant. This technique has the advantage that the magnet required for forming the particle orbits is much smaller than that needed in a cyclotron to produce the same particle energies. The acceleration is effected by radio-frequency voltages, while the synchronism is maintained by the principle of phase stability. The rate of increase of the energy of the particles is set by the rate of increase of the magnetic field strength. The peak accelerating voltage is ordinarily about twice as large as the average energy gain per turn would require, to provide the margin for phase stability. Particles can be stably accelerated with a range of energies and phases with respect to the accelerating voltage, and very intense beams can be produced.

The magnetic field must be shaped so as to focus the beam of particles. In early synchrotrons the field was caused to decrease slightly with increasing radius, as in a betatron. This arrangement resulted in a weak focusing effect that was adequate for machines in which the dimensions of the magnet gap could be appreciable in comparison with the radius of the orbit. The magnitude of the magnetic fields that may be used is limited by the saturation of the iron components that shape the field and provide a path for the magnetic flux. Therefore, if the energy of accelerators is to be increased, their radius must be increased correspondingly. For relativistic particles the radius is proportional to the kinetic energy. The magnet of a synchrotron with weak focusing, designed to have a reasonable intensity, would have a mass proportional to the cube of the radius. It is clear that increasing the energy beyond some point—in practice, about 10 GeV—would be very expensive.

The introduction of alternating-gradient focusing provided the solution to this problem and made possible the development of synchrotrons with much higher energies. The idea was promptly incorporated in the design of the 33-GeV proton synchrotron at the Brookhaven National Laboratory in Upton, N.Y., and the 28-GeV machine at the European Organization for Nuclear Research (CERN), near Geneva.

The magnetic fields in an alternating-gradient synchrotron vary much more strongly with radius than those used for weak focusing. A magnet with pole-tips curved outward from the core of the magnet produces a magnetic field that sharply decreases with increasing radius. To the particle beam, this magnetic field acts like a lens with an extrememly short focal length. In the vertical direction (the orbital plane is horizontal) it focuses the beam, but in the radial direction it is almost equally defocusing. A magnet with the pole-tip shapes curved inward to the core of the magnet produces a field that strongly increases with increasing radius. This field is defocusing in the vertical direction and focusing in the radial direction. Although pairing such magnetic fields results in partial cancellation, the overall effect is to provide focusing in both directions. The ring of magnetic field

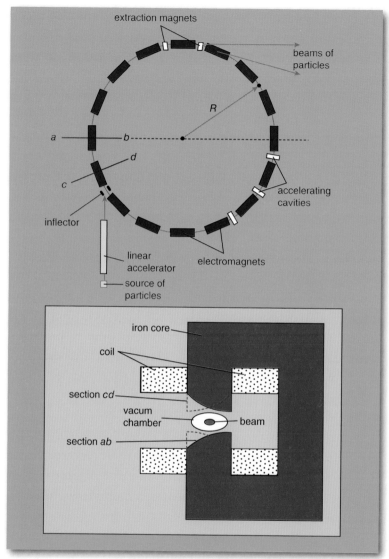

Schematic diagram of a synchrotron with alternating-gradient focusing. Particles are injected into the synchrotron ring (shown at top) *with their energies already raised by a linear accelerator. They are further accelerated around the synchrotron by a series of electromagnets, whose applied fields grow stronger as the speed of the particles rises. The beam of particles is focused by the pole-tips of the magnets, shown in cross section at bottom. Tips with cross section* cd *focus the beam in the radial direction, while tips with cross section* ab *focus in the vertical direction.* Copyright Encyclopædia Britannica; rendering for this edition by Rosen Educational Services is created by a large number of magnets, with the two types of pole-tips alternating, as shown at the top of the figure. The beam, in effect, passes through a succession of lenses as the particles move around the ring, producing a large beam current in a vacuum chamber of small cross section.

Particles accelerated in a large synchrotron are commonly injected by a linear accelerator and are steered into the ring by a device called an inflector. They begin their acceleration in the ring when the magnetic field is small. As the field created by the ring magnets increases, the injection pulse is timed so that the field and the energy of the particles from the linear accelerator are properly matched. The radio-frequency accelerating devices, usually called cavities, operate on the same principle as a short section of a linear accelerator. The useful beam may be either the accelerated particles that have been extracted from the ring by special magnets or secondary particles ejected from a target that is introduced into the beam.

ELECTRON SYNCHROTRONS

The invention of the synchrotron immediately solved the problem of the limit on the acceleration of electrons that had been imposed by the radiation of electrons moving in circular orbits. This radiation has been named synchrotron radiation because it was first observed during the operation of a 70-MeV electron synchrotron built at the General Electric Company Research and Development Center laboratory in Schenectady, N.Y. A betatron can accelerate electrons to 300 MeV only if the radiation is carefully compensated, but a synchrotron needs only a modest increase in the radio-frequency accelerating voltage. As the particles lose energy by radiation, their average phase with respect to the accelerating voltage simply shifts slightly so as to increase their average energy gain per revolution.

Electron synchrotrons with energies near 300 MeV have been constructed in several countries, the first being the one built in 1949 at Berkeley under Edwin McMillan's direction. In these accelerators the electrons were injected by a pulsed electron gun, and the initial acceleration from 50–100 keV to 2–3 MeV was induced as in a betatron. The magnets were specifically designed to provide the accelerating flux in the initial part of the magnet cycle. During this time the speed of the electrons increased from about 50 percent of the speed of light to more than 95 percent. At this point, acceleration by the radio-frequency cavity supervened, and the small further change in speed was accommodated by a 5 percent change in the radius of the orbit.

Strong focusing was first applied to the electron synchrotron in the 1.2-GeV device built in 1954 at Cornell University in Ithaca, N.Y. All large electron synchrotrons are now equipped with linear accelerators as injectors. The practical limit on the energy of an electron synchrotron is set by the cost of the radio-frequency system needed to restore the energy the electrons lose by radiation. To minimize this energy loss, the acceleration time is made as short as possible (a few milliseconds), and the magnetic fields are kept weak. The weak fields keep down the energy loss by guiding the electrons on gently curved paths. However, because synchrotron radiation losses increase as the fourth power of the energy, small increases in energy lead to large increases in radius.

The largest electron synchrotrons, used in particle physics research, operate as colliding-beam storage rings. At CERN the Large Electron-Positron (LEP) collider was designed to accelerate electrons and positrons initially to 50 GeV and later to about 100 GeV in a ring with a circumference of 27 km (17 miles). This is probably the practical limit for such machines.

Another way to reduce the energy used in an electron synchrotron is to employ superconducting radio-frequency accelerating cavities. These have no electrical resistance and hence much lower losses due to current heating effects. They are used, for example, to accelerate electrons in the 6.3-km (3.9-mile) ring of the electron-proton collider at the DESY (German Electron Synchrotron) laboratory in Hamburg, Ger. Superconducting cavities were also used to double the energy of the beams in LEP from 50 GeV per beam with copper cavities to a little over 100 GeV with superconducting cavities.

PROTON SYNCHROTRONS

The mode of operation of a proton synchrotron is very similar to that of an electron synchrotron, but there are two important differences. First, because the speed of a proton does not approach the speed of light until its energy is well above 1 GeV, the frequency of the accelerating voltage must be modulated to keep it proportional to the speed of the particle during the initial stage of the acceleration. Second, protons do not lose a significant amount of energy by radiation at energies attainable by present-day techniques. The limit on the energy of a proton synchrotron is therefore set by the cost of the magnet ring, which increases only as the first power of the energy or even more slowly. The highest-energy particle accelerators yet built are proton synchrotrons.

The first proton synchrotron to operate (1952) was the 3-GeV Cosmotron at Brookhaven. It, and other accelerators that soon followed, had weakly focusing magnets. The 28-GeV proton synchrotron at CERN and the 33-GeV machine at Brookhaven made use of the principle of alternating-gradient focusing, but not without complications. Such focusing is so strong that the time required for a particle to complete one orbit does not depend strongly on the energy of the particle. Therefore, for the energy range (which may extend to several GeV) within which acceleration appreciably affects the speed of the particle, phase stability operates as it does in a linear accelerator: the region of stable phase is on the rising side of the time curve of the accelerating voltage. At higher energies, however, the speed of the proton is substantially constant, and the region of stable phase is on the falling side of the voltage curve, as it is in a synchrocyclotron. At the point that divides these regions, called the transition energy, there is no phase stability. At Brookhaven a model electron accelerator was built to demonstrate that the beam could be accelerated through the transition energy in a stable manner.

In 1972 a large proton synchrotron went into operation at Fermilab. This machine had a magnet ring occupying a circular tunnel 6.3 km (3.9 miles) in circumference. At first it accelerated protons to 200 GeV, but by 1976 it had reached 500 GeV. In the same year, a similar accelerator, the Super Proton Synchrotron (SPS), began operation at CERN. The SPS was fed protons by the 28-GeV proton synchrotron (PS) and accelerated them to 400 GeV, reaching 450 GeV at a later date.

To reach still higher energies, Fermilab built a second synchrotron in the 6.3-km tunnel. The Tevatron was designed to operate at nearly 1,000 GeV, or 1 TeV, the energy that gives the device its name. The intense magnetic fields needed to guide and focus such an energetic proton beam are provided by 1,000 magnets with windings made of a superconducting alloy, and the whole ring is kept at 4.5 kelvins by liquid helium. The original synchrotron at Fermilab, based on conventional magnets, served as injector for the Tevatron until 1997. In 1999 the Main Injector, a new synchrotron with a 3.3-km (2.1-mile) magnet ring, replaced the earlier machine to provide a more-intense beam for the Tevatron.

At Fermilab the proton beam, initially in the guise of negative hydrogen ions (each a single proton with two electrons), originates in a 750-kV Cockcroft-Walton generator and is accelerated to 400 MeV in a linear accelerator. A carbon foil then strips the electrons from the ions, and the protons are injected into the Booster, a small synchrotron 150 metres (500 feet) in diameter, which accelerates the particles to 8 GeV. From the Booster the protons are transferred to the Main Injector, where they are further accelerated to 150 GeV before being fed to the final stage of acceleration in the Tevatron.

Until 2000, protons at 800 GeV were extracted from the Tevatron and directed onto targets to yield a variety of particle beams for different experiments. The Main Injector then became the principal machine for providing extracted beams, at the lower energy of 120 GeV but at much higher intensities than the Tevatron provided. In 1987 the Tevatron began to operate as a proton-antiproton collider, and this has been its sole function since 2000.

The SPS at CERN has also operated as proton-antiproton collider and has accelerated heavy ions (such as sulfur and lead ions), as well as electrons and positrons, for injection into the LEP collider. Together with the smaller PS, it continues to form part of CERN's integrated complex of accelerators.

COLLIDING-BEAM STORAGE RINGS

Although particles are sometimes accelerated in storage rings, the main purpose of these rings is to make possible energetic interactions between beams of particles moving in opposite directions. When a moving object strikes an identical object that is at rest, at most half of the kinetic energy of the moving object is available to produce heat or to deform the objects. The remainder is accounted for by the motions of the objects after the encounter. If, how-ever, the two objects are in motion in opposite directions with equal speeds, then all the kinetic energy is available to produce heat or deformation at the instant of collision. If the objects stick together, the combination is at rest after the collision. For particles with speeds close to that of light, the effect is accentuated. If a 400-GeV proton strikes a proton at rest, only 27.4 GeV are available for the interaction. The remainder produces motion of the par-ticles. On the other hand, if two 31.4-GeV protons collide, 62.3 GeV are available for the interaction (the collision is not quite "head-on").

In a target of liquid or solid matter, the number of par-ticles per unit volume accessible to an accelerated beam is large, but, when the target of one beam is another beam, the number of particles interacting is much smaller: the rate of interactions is proportional to the product of the currents in the two beams. Donald W. Kerst, builder of the first betatron, realized in 1956 that, though the beam current in a high-energy accelerator is small, the currents circulating in the magnet rings are effectively much larger because of the high orbital frequency of the particles. Thus, if the colliding beams are circulating in such rings, useful experiments on the interactions can be carried out. In a colliding-beam apparatus the two beams may be made up of identical particles (e.g., two beams of protons), in which case the installation consists of two separate rings of magnets. In one ring the magnetic fields guide the par-ticles clockwise. In the other the fields are oriented in the opposite direction so as to guide the particles coun-terclockwise. The rings intersect at "interaction regions," where the beams collide. In other cases the two beams are composed of particles of opposite charge (e.g., electrons and positrons, or protons and antiprotons). Such beams cir-culate in opposite directions in the same vacuum chamber, guided by the same magnets. The particles are bunched so that they collide only in the interaction regions.

The highest interaction energies at present are, and in the future will be, achieved in colliding-beam storage rings. This places the research with them at the very forefront of the quest for knowledge, even though many types of experiments cannot be conducted with storage rings. This is true partly because the number of interactions in a storage ring is a small fraction of that occurring in a stationary target and partly because storage beams do not produce intense beams of secondary particles.

ELECTRON STORAGE RINGS

Many storage rings have been constructed to study the interactions of electrons with positrons. The principal centres of this research are Cornell University; Stanford University; CERN; Tsukuba, Japan; Frascati, Italy; Beijing, China; and Novosibirsk, Russia.

Electrons are emitted from a heated filament and accelerated first in a linear accelerator and then in a synchrotron before being injected into a storage ring. To make positrons, a target such as a tungsten plate is inserted at a point along the linear accelerator. The energetic electrons radiate gamma rays in the heavy target, and these gamma rays can create electron-positron pairs. The positrons, which have positive charge, are selected by a suitable magnetic field and accelerated along the remainder of the linear accelerator. They are then fed into the synchrotron for further acceleration and finally injected into the storage ring. Since they have opposite electric charges, the electrons and positrons circulate in opposite directions through the magnets of a single storage ring.

Electron-positron storage rings are used principally for research into subatomic particles. If a single storage ring is used, the two beams will always have the same energy. Because of the pulsed operation of the acceleration system, the particles are stored in bunches, which can be made to collide at only a few places around the ring. Detectors surround one or more of the collision points to record the particles produced when an electron and a positron annihilate. Separate storage rings are sometimes used, in particular if the electrons and positrons are to have different energies. In the PEP-II storage rings at Stanford University and in the KEK-B facility at the National Laboratory for High Energy Physics (KEK) in Tsukuba, electrons and positrons are stored at different energies so that they have different values of momentum. When they annihilate, the net momentum is not zero, as it is with particles of equal and opposite momentum, so new short-lived particles (specifically, B-mesons) are created in motion. This gives them an apparently longer lifetime in the laboratory owing to the effect of time dilation in the theory of special relativity.

The highest-energy electron-positron collider built so far was the LEP machine at CERN, which operated from 1989 to 2001. LEP reached a maximum of a little over 100 GeV per beam in a magnet ring that was 27 km (17 miles) in circumference and that occupied a 4-metre- (13-foot-) wide tunnel lying, on average, 100 metres (330 feet) underground. Other accelerators built earlier at CERN acted as injectors to LEP in a complex interlinked system. A purpose-built linear accelerator produced bunches of electrons and positrons at 600 MeV and fed them into the 28-GeV proton synchrotron, where they were accelerated to 3.5 GeV. They were then transferred to the SPS for acceleration to 20 GeV before injection into LEP. In the final stage LEP accelerated the counterrotating beams of electrons and positrons to a maximum energy of just over 100 GeV. The beams were then made to collide at four points around the ring where detectors were located.

The electrons and positrons in a storage ring emit synchrotron radiation at very great rates—more than a megawatt in some installations. From a high-energy storage ring, the wavelength of this radiation extends into the X-ray region. These storage rings now constitute the brightest sources of electromagnetic radiation available in the ultraviolet and X-ray regions. This radiation is proving to be increasingly useful for research in solid-state physics, biophysics, and chemical physics. A few electron storage rings of relatively low energy are equipped with magnetic structures specially designed to bend the beam to produce synchrotron radiation and are operated solely for this purpose.

PROTON STORAGE RINGS

In 1971 CERN pioneered the storage of protons with the Intersecting Storage Rings (ISR), in which two interlaced rings each stored protons at 31 GeV. The two beams collided at eight crossing points, giving a total collision energy of 62 GeV. This was equivalent to a stationary target being struck by a beam of 2 TeV.

A decade later CERN reached much higher energies with a radical new technique, colliding protons with antiprotons that were accelerated and stored together in the ring of the 450-GeV Super Proton Synchrotron. Protons and antiprotons, having opposite electric charge, circulate in opposite directions around the same synchrotron ring. The creation of an intense beam of antiprotons requires a technique known as "stochastic cooling," developed by Simon Van der Meer at CERN. Antiprotons are produced when a high-energy proton beam strikes a metal target, but they emerge from the target with a range of energies and directions, so the resulting antiproton beam is broad and diffuse. Stochastic cooling provides a means of successively applying small correcting forces to the particles in the broad beam until they have been "cooled"—focused into a narrow beam of uniform energy. The technique is to store the particles in a large-aperture ring and use electronic devices to sense the average deviations from the desired orbit and apply an appropriate average correction at a later stage around the ring. The correction signals cross the ring directly on straight paths, so they arrive in time to influence the particles, which are traveling along a longer curved path.

The highest-energy proton-antiproton collider is the Tevatron at Fermilab. The antiprotons are produced by directing protons at 120 GeV from the Main Injector at Fermilab onto a nickel target. The antiprotons are separated from other particles produced in the collisions at the target and are focused by a lithium lens before being fed into a ring called the debuncher, where they undergo stochastic cooling. They are passed on first to an accumulator ring and then to the Recycler ring, where they are stored until there are a sufficient number for injection into the Main Injector. This provides acceleration to 150 GeV before transfer to the Tevatron. Protons and antiprotons are accelerated simultaneously in the Tevatron to about 1 TeV, in counterrotating beams. Having reached their maximum energy, the two beams are stored and then allowed to collide at points around the ring where detectors are situated to capture particles produced in the collisions.

During storage in the Tevatron, the beams gradually spread out so that collisions become less frequent. The beams are "dumped" in a graphite target at this stage, and fresh beams are made. This process wastes up to 80 percent of the antiprotons, which are difficult to make, so, when the Main Injector was built, a machine to retrieve and store the old antiprotons was also built. The Recycler, located in the same tunnel as the Main Injector, is a storage ring built from 344 permanent magnets. Because there is no need to vary the energy of the antiprotons at this stage, the magnetic field does not need to change. The use of permanent magnets saves energy costs. The Recycler "cools" the old antiprotons from the Tevatron and also reintegrates with them a new antiproton beam from the accumulator. The more-intense antiproton beams produced by the Recycler double the number of collisions in the Tevatron.

The difficulty in making intense beams of antiprotons has led CERN to return to the concept of a proton-proton collider. CERN began building the Large Hadron Collider, or LHC, in 2001, and test operations began in 2008. The LHC replaced LEP in its 27-km- (17-mile-) circumference tunnel in order to accelerate proton beams to 7 TeV. It uses a single ring of superconducting magnets of a special "2 in 1" design that bends protons in opposite directions in two separate beam pipes within the same structure. It is also designed to collide beams of heavy ions. In 2009 the LHC became the world's highest-energy particle accelerator when it produced proton beams with energies of 1.18 TeV.

At the Brookhaven National Laboratory in Upton, N.Y., the Relativistic Heavy Ion Collider (RHIC) came into operation in 2000. This has two rings of magnets that cross to accelerate beams of gold ions to 50 GeV and then bring them into head-on collision. The aim is to study quark-gluon plasma, a state of matter that is presumed to have existed in the very early universe.

ELECTRON-PROTON STORAGE RINGS

The Hadron-Electron Ring Accelerator (HERA) at the DESY laboratory stores both electrons and protons. It is the only machine that operates in this way with particles of different masses. To do so requires two interlaced rings: one to accelerate and store the electrons, the other to accelerate and store the protons. The machine, which began operation in 1992, occupies a tunnel 6.3 km (4 miles) in circumference. With high fields generated by superconducting magnets, the proton ring can reach energies up to 820 GeV. The electron energy, however, is limited by synchrotron radiation losses but reaches a maximum 30 GeV with the aid of low-loss superconducting accelerating cavities.

IMPULSE ACCELERATORS

Primarily for use in research on thermonuclear fusion of hydrogen isotopes, several high-intensity electron accelerators have been constructed. One type resembles a string of beads in which each bead is a torus of laminated iron and the string is the vacuum tube. The iron toruses constitute the cores of pulse transformers, and the beam of electrons in effect forms the secondary windings of all of the transformers, which are connected in series. The primaries are all connected in parallel and are powered by the discharge of a large bank of capacitors. These accelerators produce electron beams with energies between 1 and 9 MeV and currents between 200 and 200,000 amperes. The pulses are very brief, lasting about 50 nanoseconds. Besides their application to thermonuclear fusion, such accelerators are utilized for flash radiography, research on collective ion acceleration, microwave production, and laser excitation.

FAMOUS PARTICLE ACCELERATORS

The greatest discoveries in particle physics have been made using particle accelerators. Some of the most famous are discussed in the following sections.

ARGONNE NATIONAL LABORATORY

Argonne National Laboratory was the first U.S. national research laboratory, located in Argonne, Ill., some 40 km (25 miles) southwest of Chicago, and operated by the University of Chicago for the U.S. Department of Energy. It was founded in 1946 to conduct basic nuclear physics research and to develop the technology for peaceful uses of nuclear energy. Argonne National Laboratory now supports more than 200 basic and applied research programs—in science, engineering, and technology—that are directed to maintain basic scientific leadership, guide energy-resource development, improve nuclear-energy technology, and promote environmental-risk management.

The Argonne laboratory houses several major research facilities that are available for collaborative and interdisciplinary use by government, academic, and industrial scientists. Four of these facilities—the Advanced Photon Source (APS), the Intense Pulsed Neutron Source (IPNS), the Argonne Tandem Linear Accelerator System (ATLAS), and the High-Voltage Electron Microscope- (HVEM-) Tandem Facility—have been designated official U.S. Department of Energy National User Facilities.

The APS, which opened in 1996, is a 7-gigaelectron volt (GeV) synchrotron particle accelerator that is designed to produce brilliant (highly collimated) and intense beams of high-energy X-ray synchrotron radiation for advanced X-ray imaging and diffraction studies. Using the APS, scientists have performed X-ray diffraction analyses to unravel the structures of complex biological supramolecular assemblies, including ribosomes, enzyme-inhibitor (drug) complexes, and bacterial toxins.

ATLAS is a superconducting linear accelerator that accelerates beams of heavy ions up to and including uranium for high-energy nuclear physics research. One

Aerial view of the Argonne National Laboratory in Argonne, Ill. Argonne National Laboratory

example of this work involves experiments to probe the details of nuclear structure to answer fundamental questions concerning nuclear stability. The IPNS provides a powerful source of neutrons for neutron-scattering experiments in materials science research. Applications include high-temperature ceramics and advanced superconducting materials. The HVEM-Tandem Facility combines electron microscopy with ion-beam irradiation to study, for example, high-temperature superconductors.

CERN AND THE LARGE HADRON COLLIDER

CERN (Conseil Européen pour la Recherche Nucléaire, or in English, European Organization for Nuclear Research) is an international scientific organization established for the purpose of collaborative research into high-energy particle physics. Founded in 1954, the organization maintains its headquarters near Geneva and operates expressly for research of a "pure scientific and fundamental character." Article 2 of the CERN Convention, emphasizing the atmosphere of freedom in which CERN was established, states that it "shall have no concern with work for military requirements and the results of its experimental and theoretical work shall be published or otherwise made generally available." CERN's scientific-research facilities—representing the world's largest machines, particle accelerators, dedicated to studying the universe's smallest objects, subatomic particles—attract thousands of scientists from around the world. Research achievements at CERN, which include Nobel Prize–winning scientific discoveries, also encompass technological breakthroughs such as the World Wide Web.

The establishment of CERN was at least in part an effort to reclaim the European physicists who had immigrated for various reasons to the United States as a result of World War II. The provisional organization, which was created in 1952 as the Conseil Européen pour la Recherche Nucléaire, had been proposed in 1950 by the American physicist Isidor Isaac Rabi at the fifth General Conference of UNESCO. Upon formal ratification of the group's constitution in 1954, the word *Organisation* replaced *Conseil* in its name, although the organization continued to be known by the acronym of the earlier name. By the end of the 20th century, CERN had a membership of 20 European states, in addition to several countries that maintained "observer" status.

CERN has the largest and most-versatile facilities of its kind in the world. The site covers more than 100 hectares (250 acres) in Switzerland and, since 1965, more than 450 hectares (1,125 acres) in France. The activation in 1957 of CERN's first particle accelerator, a 600-megaelectron volt (MeV) synchrocyclotron, enabled physicists to observe (some 22 years after the prediction of this activity) the decay of a pi-meson, or pion, into an electron and a neutrino. The event was instrumental in the development of the theory of the weak force.

The CERN laboratory grew steadily, activating the particle accelerator known as the Proton Synchrotron (PS; 1959), which used "strong focusing" of particle beams to achieve 28-gigaelectron volt (GeV) acceleration of protons; the Intersecting Storage Rings (ISR; 1971), a revolutionary design enabling head-on collisions between two intense 32-GeV beams of protons to increase the effective energy available in the particle accelerator; and the Super Proton Synchrotron (SPS; 1976), which featured a 7-km (4.35-mile) circumference ring able to accelerate protons to a peak energy of 500 GeV. Experiments at the PS in 1973 demonstrated for the first time that neutrinos could interact with matter without changing into muons. This historic discovery, known as the "neutral current interaction," opened the door to the new physics embodied in the electroweak theory, uniting the weak force with the more-familiar electromagnetic force.

In 1981 the SPS was converted into a proton-antiproton collider based on the addition of an Antiproton Accumulator (AA) ring, which allowed the accumulation of antiprotons in concentrated beams. Analysis of proton-antiproton collision experiments at an energy of 270 GeV per beam led to the discovery of the W and Z particles (carriers of the weak force) in 1983. Physicist Carlo Rubbia and engineer Simon van der Meer of CERN were awarded the 1984 Nobel Prize for Physics in recognition of their contribution to this discovery, which provided experimental verification of the electroweak theory in the Standard Model of particle physics. In 1992 Georges Charpak of CERN received the Nobel Prize for Physics

THE BRITANNICA GUIDE TO PARTICLE PHYSICS

in acknowledgment of his 1968 invention of the multiwire proportional chamber, an electronic particle detector that revolutionized high-energy physics and has applications in medical physics.

The founding mission of CERN, to promote collaboration between scientists from many different countries, required for its implementation the rapid transmission and communication of experimental data to sites all over the world. In the 1980s Tim Berners-Lee, an English computer scientist at CERN, began work on a hypertext system for linking electronic documents and on the protocol for transferring them between computers. His system, introduced to CERN in 1990, became known as the World Wide Web, a means of rapid and efficient communication that transformed not only the high-energy physics community but also the entire world.

In 1989 CERN inaugurated the Large Electron-Positron (LEP) collider, with a circumference of almost 27 km (17 miles), which was able to accelerate both electrons and positrons to 45 GeV per beam (increased to 104 GeV per beam by 2000). LEP facilitated extremely precise measurements of the Z particle, which led to substantial refinements in the Standard Model. LEP was shut down in 2000 and was replaced in the same tunnel by the Large Hadron Collider (LHC), designed to collide proton beams at an energy of almost 7 teraelectron volts (TeV) per beam. The LHC, expected to extend the reach of high-energy physics experiments to a new energy plateau and thus reveal new, uncharted areas of study, began test operations in 2008.

The LHC is the world's most powerful particle accelerator. The LHC's tunnel is circular and is located 50–175 metres (165–575 feet) below ground, on the border between France and Switzerland. The LHC ran its first test operation on Sept. 10, 2008. An electrical problem in a cooling system on September 18 resulted in a temperature increase of about 100 °C (180 °F) in the magnets, which are meant to operate at temperatures near absolute zero (-273.15 °C, or -459.67 °F). Early estimates that the LHC would be quickly fixed soon turned out to be overly optimistic. It restarted on Nov. 20, 2009. Shortly thereafter, on Nov. 30, 2009, it supplanted the Fermi National Accelerator Laboratory's Tevatron as the most powerful particle accelerator, when it boosted protons to energies of 1.18 teraelectron volts (TeV; 1×10^{12} electron volts). In March 2010 scientists at CERN announced that a problem with the design of superconducting wire in the LHC required that the collider could only run at half-energy (7 TeV) until the end of 2011. The LHC is scheduled to be shut down in 2012 to fix the problem and is expected to run at its full energy of 14 TeV in 2013.

The heart of the LHC is a ring that runs through the circumference of the LEP tunnel. The ring is only a few centimetres in diameter, evacuated to a higher degree than deep space and cooled to within two degrees of absolute zero. In this ring, two counter-rotating beams of heavy ions or protons are accelerated to speeds within one millionth of a percent of the speed of light. (Protons belong to a category of heavy subatomic particles known as hadrons, which accounts for the name of this particle accelerator.) At four points on the ring, the beams can intersect and a small proportion of particles crash into each other. At maximum power, collisions between protons will take place at a combined energy of up to 14 TeV, about seven times greater than has been achieved previously. At each collision point are huge magnets weighing tens of thousands of tons and banks of detectors to collect the particles produced by the collisions.

The project took a quarter of a century to realize. Planning began in 1984, and the final go-ahead was granted in 1994. Thousands of scientists and engineers from dozens of countries were involved in designing, planning, and building the LHC, and the cost for materials and manpower was nearly $5 billion. This does not include the cost of running experiments and computers.

One goal of the LHC project is to understand the fundamental structure of matter by recreating the extreme conditions that occurred in the first few moments of the universe according to the big bang model. For decades physicists have used the so-called standard model for fundamental particles, which has worked well but has weaknesses. First, and most important, it does not explain why some particles have mass. In the 1960s British physicist Peter Higgs postulated a particle that had interacted with other particles at the beginning of time to provide them with their mass. The Higgs particle has never been observed—it should be produced only by collisions in an energy range not available for experiments before the LHC. Second, the standard model requires some arbitrary assumptions, which some physicists have suggested may be resolved by postulating a further class of supersymmetric particles—these might be produced by the extreme energies of the LHC. Finally, examination of asymmetries between particles and their antiparticles may provide a clue to another mystery: the imbalance between matter and antimatter in the universe.

As with all groundbreaking experiments, the most exciting results may well be unexpected ones. As British physicist Stephen Hawking said, "It is more exciting if we don't find the Higgs. That will show that something is wrong and we need to think again."

DESY

The Deutsches Elektronen-synchrotron (DESY, or in English, German Electron Synchrotron) is the largest centre for high-energy particle-physics research in Germany. DESY, founded in 1959, is located in Hamburg and is funded jointly by the German federal government and the city of Hamburg. Its particle-accelerator facilities are an international resource, serving thousands of physicists and scientists representing more than 30 countries around the world. DESY currently supports research initiatives in three major areas: the design and construction of particle accelerators, the characteristics of high-energy subatomic particles, and the applications of synchrotron radiation.

The first DESY particle accelerator was an electron synchrotron, completed in 1964, which was able to accelerate electrons to an energy level of 7.4 gigaelectron volts (GeV; 7.4 billion electron volts). The Double Ring Storage Facility (DORIS), completed 10 years later, was designed to collide beams of electrons and positrons at energies of 3.5 GeV per beam (upgraded to 5 GeV per beam in 1978). Now in its third version as DORIS III, this machine is no longer used as a collider. Its electron beam serves as a source of synchrotron radiation (mainly at X-ray and ultraviolet wavelengths) for the Hamburg Synchrotron Radiation Laboratory (HASYLAB). HASYLAB is a national user research facility administered within DESY that invites scientists to explore the applications of synchrotron-radiation research in molecular biology, materials science, chemistry, geophysics, and medicine.

In 1978 DESY completed construction of the Positron-Electron Tandem Ring Accelerator (PETRA), a larger collider capable of reaching 19 GeV per beam. In 1979 experiments with PETRA yielded the first direct evidence for the existence of gluons, the messenger particles of the strong force that bind quarks together within protons and neutrons. PETRA now serves as a preaccelerator for the laboratory's newest facility, the Hadron-Electron

Ring Accelerator (HERA), which was completed in 1992. HERA is the only particle accelerator capable of bringing about collisions between beams of electrons or positrons and beams of protons. HERA consists of two rings in a single tunnel with a circumference of 6.3 km (3.9 miles). One ring accelerates electrons or positrons to 30 GeV. The other, protons to 820 GeV. It is being used to unlock the inner structure of the proton—to study the energy and range at which gluons interact with quarks within the proton and to explore how the combination of quarks within the proton gives rise to its observed spin.

Physicists at DESY, in collaboration with American and Swedish research groups, participate in the Antarctic Muon and Neutrino Detector Array (AMANDA) research project at the South Pole. AMANDA utilizes thousands of photomultiplier-tube detectors—installed at a depth of 2 km (1.2 miles) beneath the surface of the Antarctic ice—to observe the weak interactions with matter of neutrinos emitted by high-energy cosmic-ray sources.

FERMI NATIONAL ACCELERATOR LABORATORY

The Fermi National Accelerator Laboratory, or Fermilab, is a U.S. national particle-accelerator laboratory and centre for particle-physics research, located in Batavia, Ill., about 43 km (27 miles) west of Chicago. The facility is operated for the U.S. Department of Energy by the Universities Research Association, a consortium of 85 research universities in the United States and four universities representing Canada, Italy, and Japan. Fermilab was founded in the mid-1960s in response to a 1963 recommendation by the Atomic Energy Commission to build a national particle-accelerator facility to conduct world-class research in nuclear physics. The Batavia site, which extends over 2,800 hectares (6,800 acres), was selected in

1966 and formally occupied in 1968. Fermilab attracts scientists from almost every U.S. state and from 45 countries worldwide for collaborative research into the fundamental nature of matter, the field of subatomic particles.

Fermilab's first particle accelerator was a proton synchrotron, a cyclic accelerator with a ring circumference of 6.3 km (3.9 miles). It began operation in 1972 and could accelerate protons to 400 gigaelectron volts (GeV; 400 billion electron volts). In the 1980s a second and more-powerful particle accelerator, the Tevatron, was constructed in the same tunnel but below the original synchrotron ring. The Tevatron was the world's highest-energy particle accelerator until 2009, when it was supplanted by the Large Hadron Collider of the European Organization for Nuclear Research (CERN).

In 1977 a Fermilab team led by American physicist Leon Lederman, studying the results of 400-GeV proton-nucleus collisions in the original main ring, discovered the first evidence for the upsilon meson, which revealed the existence of the bottom quark. The bottom quark, the fifth quark to be detected, is a member of the third and heaviest pair of quarks. The companion particle of this pair is the top quark, which is the sixth and most massive quark, and it was also discovered at Fermilab in 1995. Scientists inferred the existence of the top quark, produced in the Tevatron as a result of 1.8-TeV proton-antiproton collisions, on the basis of its decay characteristics. In 2010 scientists used the Tevatron to detect a slight preference for B-mesons (particles that contain a bottom quark) to decay into muons rather than anti-muons. This violation of charge symmetry could lead to an explanation for why there is more matter than antimatter in the universe.

The Fermilab site, consisting of thousands of hectares of undeveloped land, offers a prime opportunity to study and restore a native prairie ecosystem. Since 1975 Fermilab has been engaged in a wide-ranging prairie-restoration project—restoring native prairie grasses to the area, maintaining a herd of bison on the grounds, and establishing a waterfowl habitat. In 1989 Fermilab was recognized as a National Environmental Research Park, a protected outdoor laboratory for ecological studies.

SLAC

The Stanford Linear Accelerator Center (SLAC) is a U.S. national particle-accelerator laboratory for research in high-energy particle physics and synchrotron-radiation physics, located in Menlo Park, Calif. An exemplar of post-World War II Big Science, SLAC was founded in 1962 and is run by Stanford University for the U.S. Department of Energy. Its facilities are used by scientists from across the United States and around the world to study the fundamental constituents of matter. SLAC houses the longest linear accelerator (linac) in the world—a machine 3.2 km (2 miles) long that can accelerate electrons to energies of 50 gigaelectron volts (GeV; 50 billion electron volts).

The concept of the SLAC multi-GeV electron linac evolved from the successful development of smaller electron linacs at Stanford University, which culminated in the early 1950s in a 1.2-GeV machine. In 1962 plans for the new machine, designed to reach 20 GeV, were authorized, and the 3.2-km linac was completed in 1966. In 1968 experiments at SLAC provided the first direct evidence—based on analysis of the scattering patterns observed when high-energy electrons from the linac were allowed to strike protons and neutrons in a fixed target—for internal structure (i.e., quarks) within protons and neutrons. Richard E. Taylor of SLAC shared the 1990 Nobel Prize for Physics with Jerome Isaac Friedman and Henry Way Kendall of the Massachusetts Institute of

Technology (MIT) for confirmation of the quark model of subatomic-particle structure.

The research capacity of SLAC was augmented in 1972 with the completion of the Stanford Positron-Electron Asymmetric Rings (SPEAR), a collider designed to produce and study electron-positron collisions at energies of 2.5 GeV per beam (later upgraded to 4 GeV). In 1974 physicists working with SPEAR reported the discovery of a new, heavier flavour of quark, which became known as "charm." Burton Richter of SLAC and Samuel C.C. Ting of MIT and Brookhaven National Laboratory were awarded the Nobel Prize for Physics in 1976 in recognition of this discovery. In 1975 Martin Lewis Perl studied the results of electron-positron annihilation events occurring in SPEAR experiments and concluded that a new, heavy relative of the electron—called the tau—was involved. Perl and Frederick Reines of the University of California, Irvine, shared the 1995 Nobel Prize for Physics for their contributions to the physics of the lepton class of elementary particles, to which the tau belongs.

SPEAR was followed by a larger, higher-energy colliding-beam particle accelerator, the Positron-Electron Project (PEP), which began operation in 1980 and raised electron-positron collision energies to a total of 30 GeV. As the high-energy physics program at SLAC was shifted to PEP, the SPEAR particle accelerator became a dedicated facility for synchrotron-radiation research. SPEAR now provides high-intensity X-ray beams for structural studies of a variety of materials, ranging from bones to semiconductors.

The Stanford Linear Collider (SLC) project, which became operational in 1989, consisted of extensive modifications to the original linac to accelerate electrons and positrons to 50 GeV each before sending them in opposite directions around a 600-metre (2,000-foot) loop of magnets. The oppositely charged particles were allowed to collide, which resulted in a total collision energy of 100 GeV. The increased collision energy characteristic of the SLC led to precise determinations of the mass of the Z particle, the neutral carrier of the weak force that acts on fundamental particles.

In 1998 the Stanford linac began to feed PEP-II, a machine consisting of a positron ring and an electron ring built one above the other in the original PEP tunnel. The energies of the beams are tuned to create B mesons, particles that contain the bottom quark. These are important for understanding the difference between matter and antimatter that gives rise to the phenomenon known as CP violation.

CONCLUSION

One of the most significant branches of contemporary physics is particle physics—the study of the fundamental subatomic constituents of matter, the elementary particles. This field, also called high-energy physics, emerged in the 1930s out of the developing experimental areas of nuclear and cosmic-ray physics. Initially, investigators studied cosmic rays, the very-high-energy extraterrestrial radiations that fall upon Earth and interact in the atmosphere. However, after World War II, scientists gradually began using high-energy particle accelerators to provide subatomic particles for study. Quantum field theory, a generalization of quantum electrodynamics (QED) to other types of force fields, is essential for the analysis of high-energy physics. Subatomic particles cannot be visualized as tiny analogues of ordinary material objects such as billiard balls, for they have properties that appear contradictory from the classical viewpoint. That is to say, while they possess charge, spin, mass, magnetism, and other complex characteristics, they are nonetheless regarded as pointlike.

During the latter half of the 20th century, a coherent picture evolved of the underlying strata of matter involving two types of subatomic particles: fermions (baryons and leptons), which have odd half-integral angular momentum (spin 1/2, 3/2) and make up ordinary matter, and bosons (gluons, mesons, and photons), which have integral spins and mediate the fundamental forces of physics. Leptons (e.g., electrons, muons, taus), gluons, and photons are believed to be truly fundamental particles. Baryons (e.g., neutrons, protons) and mesons (e.g., pions, kaons), collectively known as hadrons, are believed to be formed from indivisible elements known as quarks, which have never been isolated.

Quarks come in six types, or "flavours," and have matching antiparticles, known as antiquarks. Quarks have charges that are either positive two-thirds or negative one-third of the electron's charge, while antiquarks have the opposite charges. Like quarks, each lepton has an antiparticle with properties that mirror those of its partner (the antiparticle of the negatively charged electron is the positive electron, or positron; that of the neutrino is the antineutrino). In addition to their electric and magnetic properties, quarks participate in both the strong force (which binds them together) and the weak force (which underlies certain forms of radioactivity), while leptons take part in only the weak force.

Baryons, such as neutrons and protons, are formed by combining three quarks—thus baryons have a charge of -1, 0, or 1. Mesons, which are the particles that mediate the strong force inside the atomic nucleus, are composed of one quark and one antiquark. All known mesons have a charge of -2, -1, 0, 1, or 2. Most of the possible quark combinations, or hadrons, have particularly short lifetimes, and many of them have never been seen, though additional ones have been observed with each new generation of more powerful particle accelerators.

A modern unified theory of weak and electromagnetic interactions, known as the electroweak theory, proposes that the weak force involves the exchange of particles about 100 times as massive as protons. These massive quanta have been observed—namely, two charged particles, W^+ and W^-, and a neutral one, Z°.

In the theory of the strong force known as quantum chromodynamics (QCD), eight quanta, called gluons, bind quarks to form baryons and also bind quarks to antiquarks to form mesons, the force itself being dubbed the "colour force." (This unusual use of the term *colour* is a somewhat forced analogue of ordinary colour mixing.) Quarks are said to come in three colours—red, blue, and green. The gluons and quarks themselves, being coloured, are permanently confined (deeply bound within the particles of which they are a part), while the colour-neutral composites such as protons can be directly observed. One consequence of colour confinement is that the observable particles are either electrically neutral or have charges that are integral multiples of the charge of the electron. A number of specific predictions of QCD have been experimentally tested and found correct.

CHAPTER 4
BIOGRAPHIES

M any great 20th-century physicists advanced the field of particle physics. Some of their biographies are presented here.

PATRICK M.S. BLACKETT

(b. Nov. 18, 1897, London, Eng.—d. July 13, 1974, London)

Patrick Maynard Stuart Blackett, Baron Blackett of Chelsea, was the winner of the Nobel Prize for Physics in 1948 for his discoveries in the field of cosmic radiation, which he accomplished primarily with cloud-chamber photographs that revealed the way in which a stable atomic nucleus can be disintegrated by bombarding it with alpha particles (helium nuclei). Although such nuclear disintegration had been observed previously, his data explained this phenomenon for the first time and were useful in explaining disintegration by other means.

After graduating from Cambridge University in 1921, Blackett spent 10 years as a research worker in the Cavendish Laboratory. There he began to develop the Wilson cloud chamber—a device that detects the path of ionizing particles—into an automatic instrument for the study of cosmic radiation. He received the Nobel Prize for his interpretation of the data he obtained from this device.

Blackett became professor of physics at the University of London in 1933 and Langworthy professor of physics at the University of Manchester in 1937. He established a school of cosmic-ray research and stimulated the development of other research interests, which led to the creation

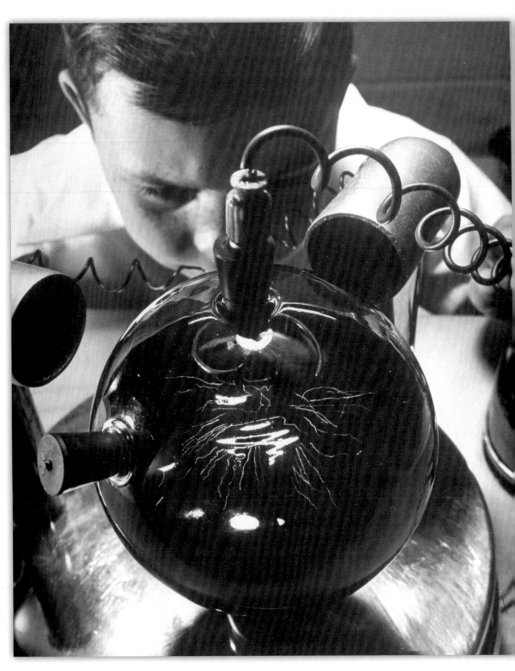

The Wilson cloud chamber detects the path of ionizing particles, but Patrick Blackett began to develop it into an automatic instrument to investigate cosmic radiation. Bernard Hoffman/Time & Life Pictures/Getty Images

of the first chair of radio astronomy at the University of Manchester, and to the building of the Jodrell Bank Experimental Station for Radio Astronomy. In 1953 he was appointed professor and head of the physics department of the Imperial College of Science and Technology in London, where he became senior research fellow in 1965. That year he was named president of the Royal Society. He was created a life peer in 1969.

SIR JAMES CHADWICK

(b. Oct. 20, 1891, Manchester, Eng.—d. July 24, 1974, Cambridge, Cambridgeshire)

English physicist Sir James Chadwick received the Nobel Prize for Physics in 1935 for the discovery of the neutron.

Educated at the universities of Manchester and Cambridge, Chadwick also studied under Hans Geiger at the Technische Hochschule, Berlin. From 1923 he worked with Ernest Rutherford in the Cavendish Laboratory, Cambridge, where they studied the transmutation of elements by bombarding them with alpha particles and investigated the nature of the atomic nucleus, identifying the proton, the nucleus of the hydrogen atom, as a constituent of the nuclei of other atoms.

In 1932 Chadwick observed that beryllium, when exposed to bombardment by alpha particles, released an unknown radiation that in turn ejected protons from the nuclei of various substances. Chadwick interpreted this radiation as being composed of particles of mass approximately equal to that of the proton, but without electrical charge—neutrons.

This discovery provided a new tool for inducing atomic disintegration, since neutrons, being electrically uncharged, could penetrate undeflected into the atomic nucleus. Chadwick was knighted in 1945.

OWEN CHAMBERLAIN

(b. July 10, 1920, San Francisco, Calif., U.S.—d. Feb. 28, 2006, Berkeley, Calif.)

American physicist Owen Chamberlain shared the Nobel Prize for Physics in 1959 with Emilio Segrè for their discovery of the antiproton. This previously postulated subatomic particle was the second antiparticle to be discovered and led directly to the discovery of many additional antiparticles.

Chamberlain attended Dartmouth College (B.A., 1941) and the University of California at Berkeley before working on the Manhattan Project, a U.S. research project that produced the first atom bombs. Later, while completing a Ph.D. (1948) at the University of Chicago, he worked at Argonne National Laboratory in Illinois. In 1948 he joined the faculty of the University of California at Berkeley, where he became a full professor in 1958 and professor emeritus in 1989. There he conducted research on alpha particle decay, neutron diffraction in liquids, and high-energy nuclear particle reactions. He and Segrè used the bevatron (a powerful particle accelerator) to produce antiprotons in 1955, and the following year they confirmed the existence of the antineutron.

SIR JOHN DOUGLAS COCKCROFT

(b. May 27, 1897, Todmorden, Yorkshire, Eng.—d. Sept. 18, 1967, Cambridge, Cambridgeshire)

Sir John Douglas Cockcroft was a British physicist and joint winner, with Ernest T.S. Walton of Ireland, of the 1951 Nobel Prize for Physics for pioneering the use of particle accelerators in studying the atomic nucleus.

Educated at the University of Manchester and St. John's College, Cambridge, Cockcroft was Jacksonian professor of natural philosophy at the University of Cambridge from 1939 to 1946. In 1932 he and Walton designed the Cockcroft-Walton generator and used it to disintegrate lithium atoms by bombarding them with protons. This type of accelerator proved to be one of the most useful in the world's laboratories. They conducted further research on the splitting of other atoms and established the importance of accelerators as a tool for nuclear research. During World War II Cockcroft was director of the Atomic Energy Division, National Research Council of Canada. In 1946 he became director of the Atomic Energy Research Establishment, Ministry of Supply, at Harwell, Berkshire, and was a chairman in the Ministry of Defence from 1952 to 1954. Cockcroft was knighted in 1948 and was created Knight Commander of the Bath in 1953. In 1960 he became master of the newly founded Churchill College at Cambridge.

RAYMOND DAVIS, JR.

(b. Oct. 14, 1914, Washington, D.C., U.S.—d. May 31, 2006, Blue Point, N.Y.)

American physicist Raymond Davis, Jr., with Koshiba Masatoshi, won the Nobel Prize for Physics in 2002 for detecting neutrinos. Riccardo Giacconi also won a share of the award for his work on X-rays.

Davis received a Ph.D. from Yale University in 1942. After military service during World War II, he joined Brookhaven National Laboratory in Upton, N.Y., in 1948. He remained there until his retirement in 1984. In 1985 Davis took a post as a research professor with the University of Pennsylvania.

Davis's prizewinning work focused on neutrinos, subatomic particles that had long baffled scientists. Since the 1920s it had been suspected that the Sun shines because

For 25 years Raymond Davis, Jr., monitored an underground tank filled with the cleaning solution tetrachloroethylene. Although he confirmed that the Sun produces neutrinos, he observed fewer than expected, a deficit known as the solar neutrino problem. Hemera/Thinkstock of nuclear fusion reactions that transform hydrogen into helium and release energy. Later, theoretical calculations indicated that countless neutrinos must be released in those reactions and, consequently, that Earth must be exposed to a constant flood of solar neutrinos. Because neutrinos interact weakly with matter, however, only one in every trillion is stopped on its way to Earth. Neutrinos thus developed a reputation for being undetectable.

Some of Davis's contemporaries had speculated that one type of nuclear reaction might produce neutrinos with enough energy to make them detectable. If such a neutrino collided with a chlorine atom, it should form a radioactive argon nucleus. In the 1960s, in a gold mine in South Dakota, Davis built an underground neutrino detector, a huge tank filled with more than 600 tons of the cleaning fluid tetrachloroethylene. He calculated that high-energy neutrinos passing through the tank should form 20 argon atoms a month on average, and he developed a way to count those exceedingly rare atoms. Monitoring the tank for more than 25 years, he was able to confirm that the Sun produces neutrinos, but he consistently found fewer neutrinos than predicted. This deficit became known as the solar neutrino problem. Davis's results were later confirmed by Koshiba, who also found evidence that neutrinos change from one type to another in flight. Because Davis's detector was sensitive to only one type, those that had switched identity eluded detection.

SHELDON GLASHOW

(b. Dec. 5, 1932, New York, N.Y., U.S.)

Sheldon Lee Glashow was an American theoretical physicist who, with Steven Weinberg and Abdus Salam, received the Nobel Prize for Physics in 1979 for their complementary efforts in formulating the electroweak theory, which explains the unity of electromagnetism and the weak force.

Glashow was the son of Jewish immigrants from Russia. He and Weinberg were members of the same classes at the Bronx High School of Science, New York City (1950), and Cornell University (1954). Glashow received his Ph.D. in physics from Harvard University in 1959. He joined the faculty of the University of California at Berkeley in 1961 and returned to Harvard as a professor of physics in 1967.

In the 1960s Weinberg and Salam had each independently devised a theory by which the weak nuclear force and the electromagnetic force could be conceived as manifestations of a single unified force called the electroweak force. Their theory could be applied only to leptons, however, a class of particles that includes electrons and neutrinos. Glashow found a way to extend their theory to other classes of elementary particles, notably baryons (e.g., protons and neutrons) and mesons. In doing so, Glashow had to invent a new property for quarks, which are the fundamental particles that constitute baryons and mesons. This new property, which Glashow called "charm," provided a valuable extension of the theory of quarks.

DAVID J. GROSS

(b. Feb. 19, 1941, Washington, D.C., U.S.)

David Jonathan Gross was an American physicist who, with H. David Politzer and Frank Wilczek, was awarded the Nobel Prize for Physics in 2004 for discoveries regarding the strong force — the nuclear force that binds together quarks (the smallest building blocks of matter) and holds together the nucleus of the atom.

Gross graduated from Hebrew University in Jerusalem in 1962 and received a Ph.D. in physics from the University of California, Berkeley, in 1966. In 1969 he joined the faculty at Princeton University, where he began working with Wilczek, then a graduate student. In 1997 Gross became director of the Kavli Institute for Theoretical Physics at the University of California, Santa Barbara.

The prizewinning work of Gross and Wilczek—and Politzer working independently—arose from physics experiments conducted in the early 1970s with particle accelerators to study quarks and the force that acts on them. During their research the three scientists observed that quarks were so tightly bound together that they could not be separated as individual particles but that the closer quarks approached one another, the weaker the strong force became. When quarks were brought very close together, the force was so weak that the quarks acted almost as if they were free particles not bound together by any force. When the distance between two quarks increased, however, the force became greater—an effect analogous to the stretching of a rubber band. This phenomenon became known as asymptotic freedom, and it led to a completely new physical theory, quantum chromodynamics (QCD), to describe the strong force. QCD enabled scientists to complete the standard model of particle physics, which describes the fundamental particles in nature and how they interact with one another.

Gross also did research in superstring theory, and in 1987 he was coinventor of a new superstring model. In addition to the Nobel Prize, Gross's numerous awards include a MacArthur Foundation fellowship (1987).

WILLIAM WEBSTER HANSEN

(b. May 27, 1909, Fresno, Calif., U.S.—d. May 23, 1949, Palo Alto, Calif.)

American physicist William Webster Hansen contributed to the development of radar and is regarded as the founder of microwave technology.

After earning a Ph.D. at Stanford University in 1933, Hansen began teaching there the next year. His early pioneering work in 1937 on microwave resonant cavities was key to the development of microwave technology just before World War II. At that time he also began work, with the brothers Russell and Sigurd Varian, on the problem of detecting aircraft. Using the technology of resonant cavities, Hansen developed the basis for a new microwave vacuum tube called the klystron amplifier, which he and the Varian brothers employed in a radar system designed for aircraft detection. The klystron has been an important device for both radar and high-energy particle accelerators used in physics research. Hansen's resonant-cavity work also led directly to the successful invention of the microwave-cavity magnetron by the British in 1940. Without Hansen's resonant cavity there likely would have been no cavity magnetron and no microwave devices available for use in World War II, and the effectiveness of radar would have been diminished significantly. Hansen published very little in the open literature, but many early publications by others on microwaves during and just after World War II acknowledge the influence of his often-quoted unpublished notes on microwaves.

In 1941 Hansen and his research group moved to the plant of the Sperry Gyroscope Company in Garden City, N.Y., contributing to developments on Doppler radar, aircraft blind-landing systems, electron acceleration, and nuclear magnetic resonance. During World War II Hansen was a scientific consultant on the Manhattan Project as well as a contributor to work on radar at the Massachusetts Institute of Technology's Radiation Laboratory. Hansen also applied his work with the resonant cavity to the design of electron accelerators used in the study of subatomic particles, though he was distracted from this pursuit by the invention of the klystron and its application to radar.

After the war, as director of Stanford's microwave laboratory, Hansen began the design of a 750-million-volt linear accelerator powered by high-power klystrons. It was completed at Stanford after his death.

GERARDUS 'T HOOFT

(b. July 5, 1946, Den Helder, Neth.)

Dutch physicist Gerardus 't Hooft was a corecipient with Martinus J.G. Veltman of the 1999 Nobel Prize for Physics for their development of a mathematical model that enabled scientists to predict the properties of both the subatomic particles that constitute the universe and the fundamental forces through which they interact. Their work facilitated the finding of a new subatomic particle, the top quark.

In 1972 't Hooft earned his doctorate in physics at the University of Utrecht and five years later became a professor there. He also was a visiting professor at numerous other institutions, including Duke and Boston universities.

'T Hooft was a student of Veltman's at the University of Utrecht, and at that time the fundamental theory of particle physics, known as the standard model, did not provide for detailed calculations of physical quantities. In the 1960s scientists had formulated the electroweak theory, which showed theoretically that two of the model's fundamental forces, electromagnetism and the weak nuclear force, could be viewed as products of a single force, termed the electroweak force. The electroweak theory was without a mathematical foundation, however, and in 1969 't Hooft and Veltman undertook to change, or "renormalize," it into a workable theory. In 1971 't Hooft published two articles that represented a major advance toward the goal. The two men then used a computer designed by Veltman to formulate the needed mathematical basis. With the information, they were able to identify the properties of the W and Z particles predicted by the theory. The 't Hooft-Veltman model allowed scientists to calculate the physical properties of other particles, including the mass of the top quark, which was directly observed in 1995.

KOSHIBA MASATOSHI
(b. Sept. 19, 1926, Toyohashi, Japan)

Japanese physicist Koshiba Masatoshi, with Raymond Davis, Jr., won the Nobel Prize for Physics in 2002 for their detection of neutrinos. Riccardo Giacconi also won a share of the award for his work on the cosmic sources of X rays.

Koshiba earned a Ph.D. from the University of Rochester in New York in 1955. He then joined the University of Tokyo, where he became professor in 1960 and emeritus professor in 1987. From 1987 to 1997 Koshiba taught at Tokai University.

Koshiba's award-winning work centred on neutrinos, subatomic particles that had long perplexed scientists. Since the 1920s it had been suspected that the Sun shines because of nuclear fusion reactions that transform hydrogen into helium and release energy. Later, theoretical calculations indicated that countless neutrinos must be released in these reactions and, consequently, that Earth must be exposed to a constant flood of solar neutrinos. Because neutrinos interact weakly with matter, however, only one in a trillion is stopped on its way to Earth. Neutrinos thus developed a reputation as being undetectable.

In the 1980s Koshiba, drawing on the work done by Davis, constructed an underground neutrino detector in a zinc mine in Japan. Called Kamiokande II, it was an enormous water tank surrounded by electronic detectors to sense flashes of light produced when neutrinos interacted with atomic nuclei in water molecules. Koshiba was able to confirm Davis's results—that the Sun produces neutrinos and that fewer neutrinos were found than had been expected (a deficit that became known as the solar neutrino problem). In 1987 Kamiokande also detected neutrinos from a supernova explosion outside the Milky Way. After building a larger, more sensitive detector named Super-Kamiokande, which became operational in 1996, Koshiba found strong evidence for what scientists had already suspected—that neutrinos, of which three types are known, change from one type into another in flight.

ERNEST ORLANDO LAWRENCE

(b. Aug. 8, 1901, Canton, S.D., U.S.—d. Aug. 27, 1958, Palo Alto, Calif.)

American physicist Ernest Orlando Lawrence was the winner of the 1939 Nobel Prize for Physics for his invention of the cyclotron, the first particle accelerator to achieve high energies.

Lawrence earned his Ph.D. at Yale University in 1925. An assistant professor of physics at Yale (1927–28), he went to the University of California, Berkeley, as an associate professor and became full professor there in 1930.

Lawrence first conceived the idea for the cyclotron in 1929. One of his students, M. Stanley Livingston, undertook the project and succeeded in building a device that accelerated hydrogen ions (protons) to an energy of 13,000 electron volts (eV). Lawrence then set out to build a second cyclotron. When completed, it accelerated protons to 1,200,000 eV, enough energy to cause nuclear disintegration. To continue the program, Lawrence built the

Radiation Laboratory at Berkeley in 1936 and was made its director.

One of Lawrence's cyclotrons produced technetium, the first element that does not occur in nature to be made artificially. His basic design was used in developing other particle accelerators, which have been largely responsible for the great advances made in the field of particle physics. With the cyclotron, he produced radioactive phosphorus and other isotopes for medical use, including radioactive iodine for the first therapeutic treatment of hyperthyroidism. In addition, he instituted the use of neutron beams in treating cancer.

During World War II he worked with the Manhattan Project as a program chief in charge of the development of the electromagnetic process of separating uranium-235 for the atomic bomb. In 1957 he received the Fermi Award

Ernest Orlando Lawrence, Berkeley, Calif. University of California, Lawrence Berkeley Lab.

from the U.S. Atomic Energy Commission. Besides his work in nuclear physics, Lawrence invented and patented a colour-television picture tube. In his honour were named Lawrence Berkeley Laboratory at Berkeley; Lawrence Livermore National Laboratory at Livermore, Calif.; and element 103, lawrencium.

TSUNG-DAO LEE

(b. Nov. 24, 1926, Shanghai, China)

Chinese-born American physicist Tsung-Dao Lee, with Chen Ning Yang, received the Nobel Prize for Physics in 1957 for work in discovering violations of the principle of parity conservation (the quality of space reflection symmetry of subatomic particle interactions), thus bringing about major refinements in particle physics theory.

In 1946 Lee was awarded a scholarship to study in the United States, and, although he had no undergraduate degree, he entered the graduate school in physics at the University of Chicago, where Enrico Fermi selected him as a doctoral student. After working briefly at the University of Chicago's Yerkes Astronomical Observatory in Wisconsin, the University of California at Berkeley, and for two years with Yang at the Institute for Advanced Study, Princeton, N.J., Lee was appointed assistant professor of physics at Columbia University in 1953.

In 1956 Lee and Yang concluded that the theta-meson and tau-meson, previously thought to be different because they decay by modes of differing parity, are in fact the same particle (now called the K-meson). Because the law of parity conservation prohibits a single particle from having decay modes exhibiting opposite parity, the only possible conclusion was that, for weak interactions at least, parity is not conserved. They suggested experiments to test their hypothesis, and in 1956–57 Chien-Shiung Wu, working at Columbia University, experimentally confirmed their theoretical conclusions.

In 1960 Lee was appointed professor of physics at the Institute for Advanced Study, and three years later he returned to Columbia to assume the first Enrico Fermi professorship in physics. From 1964 he made important contributions to the explanation of the violations of time-reversal invariance, which occur during certain weak interactions.

EDWIN MATTISON MCMILLAN

(b. Sept. 18, 1907, Redondo Beach, Calif., U.S.—d. Sept. 7, 1991, El Cerrito, Calif.)

American nuclear physicist Edwin Mattison McMillan shared the Nobel Prize for Chemistry in 1951 with Glenn T. Seaborg for his discovery of element 93, neptunium, the first element heavier than uranium, thus called a transuranium element.

McMillan was educated at the California Institute of Technology and at Princeton University, where he earned a Ph.D. in 1932. He then joined the faculty of the University of California, Berkeley, and became a full professor in 1946 and director of the Lawrence Radiation Laboratory in 1958. He retired in 1973.

While studying nuclear fission, McMillan discovered neptunium, a decay product of uranium-239. In 1940, in collaboration with Philip H. Abelson, he isolated the new element and obtained final proof of his discovery. Neptunium was the first of a host of transuranium elements that provide important nuclear fuels and contributed greatly to the knowledge of chemistry and nuclear theory. During World War II McMillan also did research on radar and sonar and worked on the first atomic bomb. He served as a member of the General Advisory Committee to the U.S. Atomic Energy Commission from 1954 to 1958.

McMillan also made a major advance in the development of Ernest Lawrence's cyclotron, which in the early 1940s had run up against its theoretical limit. Accelerated in an ever-widening spiral by synchronized electrical pulses, atomic particles in a cyclotron are unable to attain a velocity beyond a certain point, as a relativistic mass increase tends to put them out of step with the pulses. In 1945, independently of the Russian physicist Vladimir I. Veksler, McMillan found a way of maintaining synchronization for indefinite speeds. He coined the name synchrocyclotron for accelerators using this principle. McMillan was chairman of the National Academy of Sciences from 1968 to 1971.

SIMON VAN DER MEER

(b. Nov. 24, 1925, The Hague, Neth.)

In 1984 Dutch physical engineer Simon van der Meer, with Carlo Rubbia, received the Nobel Prize for Physics for his contribution to the discovery of the massive, short-lived subatomic particles designated W and Z that were crucial to the unified electroweak theory posited in the 1970s by Steven Weinberg, Abdus Salam, and Sheldon Glashow.

After receiving a degree in physical engineering from the Higher Technical School in Delft, Neth., in 1952, van der Meer worked for the Philips Company. In 1956 he joined the staff of CERN (the European Organization for Nuclear Research), near Geneva, where he remained until his retirement in 1990.

The electroweak theory provided the first reliable estimates of the masses of the W and Z particles—nearly 100 times the mass of the proton. The most promising means of bringing about a physical interaction that would release enough energy to form the particles was to cause a beam of highly accelerated protons, moving through an evacuated tube, to collide with an oppositely directed beam of antiprotons. CERN's circular particle accelerator, four miles in circumference, was the first to be converted into a colliding-beam apparatus in which the desired experiments could be performed. Manipulation of the beams required a highly effective method for keeping the particles from scattering out of the proper path and hitting the walls of the tube. Van der Meer, in response to this problem, devised a mechanism that would monitor the particle scattering at a particular point on the ring and would trigger a device on the opposite side of the ring to modify the electric fields in such a way as to keep the particles on course.

YOICHIRO NAMBU

(b. Jan. 18, 1921, Tokyo, Japan)

Japanese-born American physicist Yoichiro Nambu was awarded, with Kobayashi Makoto and Maskawa Toshihide, the 2008 Nobel Prize for Physics. Nambu received half of the prize for his discovery of spontaneous broken symmetry in subatomic physics, which explained why matter is much more common in the cosmos than antimatter. This theoretical research, which was mostly carried out in the 1960s, also earned him a share of Israel's 1995 Wolf Prize in Physics.

Nambu was one of the founders of string theory, which models subatomic particles as tiny one-dimensional "stringlike" entities. In particular, he was a pioneer in quantum chromodynamics, a field in which he first suggested that the gluon (in three "colours": red, green, and blue) is the intermediary in carrying the strong force between quarks in nucleons.

After receiving a B.S. in 1942 from the University of Tokyo, Nambu worked as a professor at Ōsaka City University. He received a doctorate in science from the University of Tokyo in 1952, and that same year he went to the United States on the invitation of the Institute for Advanced Study in Princeton, N.J. In 1954 he joined the University of Chicago as a research assistant. He became professor emeritus there in 1991.

H. DAVID POLITZER

(b. Aug. 31, 1949, New York, N.Y., U.S.)

American physicist Hugh David Politzer, with David J. Gross and Frank Wilczek, was awarded the Nobel Prize for Physics in 2004 for discoveries regarding the strong force—the nuclear force that binds together quarks (the smallest building blocks of matter) and holds together the nucleus of the atom.

Politzer studied physics at the University of Michigan (B.S., 1969) and Harvard University (Ph.D., 1974). In 1975 he began teaching at the California Institute of Technology, and from 1986 to 1988 he served as head of the school's physics department.

In the early 1970s Politzer—along with Gross and Wilczek, who were pursuing parallel research at Princeton University—used particle accelerators to study quarks and the force that acts on them. They discovered that quarks were so tightly bound together that they could not be separated as individual particles but that the closer quarks approached one another, the weaker the strong force became. When quarks were brought extremely close together, the force was so weak that the quarks acted almost as if they were free particles not bound together by any force. When the distance between two quarks increased, the force became greater—an effect analogous to the stretching of a rubber band. This phenomenon became known as asymptotic freedom, and it led to a new physical theory, quantum chromodynamics (QCD), to describe the strong force. QCD completed the standard model, a theory that describes the fundamental particles in nature and how they interact with one another.

Politzer had a featured role in the film *Fat Man and Little Boy* (1989), a fictional look at the Manhattan Project.

CARLO RUBBIA
(b. March 31, 1934, Gorizia, Italy)

Italian physicist Carlo Rubbia in 1984 shared with Simon van der Meer the Nobel Prize for Physics for the discovery of the massive, short-lived subatomic W particle and Z particle. These particles are the carriers of the so-called weak force involved in the radioactive decay of atomic nuclei. Their existence strongly confirms the validity of the electroweak theory, proposed in the 1970s, that the weak force and electromagnetism are different manifestations of a single basic kind of physical interaction.

Rubbia was educated at the Normal School of Pisa and the University of Pisa, earning a doctorate from the latter in 1957. He taught there for two years before moving to Columbia University as a research fellow. He joined the faculty of the University of Rome in 1960 and was appointed senior physicist at the European Centre for Nuclear Research (CERN; now the European Organization for Nuclear Research), Geneva, in 1962. In 1970 he was appointed professor of physics at Harvard

University and thereafter divided his time between Harvard and CERN.

In 1973 a research group under Rubbia's direction provided one of the experimental clues that led to the formulation of the electroweak theory by observing neutral weak currents (weak interactions in which electrical charge is not transferred between the particles involved). These interactions differ from those previously observed and are direct analogues of electromagnetic interactions. The electroweak theory embodied the idea that the weak force can be transmitted by any of three particles called intermediate vector bosons. Furthermore, it indicated that these particles (W^+, W^-, and Z^0) should have masses nearly 100 times that of the proton.

Rubbia then proposed that the large synchrotron at CERN be modified so that beams of accelerated protons and antiprotons could be made to collide head-on, releasing energies great enough for the weak bosons to materialize. In 1983 experiments with the colliding-beam apparatus gave proof that the W and Z particles are indeed produced and have properties that agree with the theoretical predictions.

Further analysis of the results obtained in 1983 led Rubbia to conclude that in some decays of the W^+ particle, the first firm evidence for the sixth quark, called top, had been found. The discovery of this quark confirmed an earlier prediction that three pairs of these particles should exist.

ABDUS SALAM

(b. Jan. 29, 1926, Jhang Maghiāna, Punjab, India [now in Pakistan]—d. Nov. 21, 1996, Oxford, Eng.)

Pakistani nuclear physicist Abdus Salam was the corecipient with Steven Weinberg and Sheldon Lee Glashow of the 1979 Nobel Prize for Physics for their work in formulating the electroweak theory, which explains the unity of the weak nuclear force and electromagnetism.

Salam attended the Government College at Lahore, and in 1952 he received his Ph.D. in theoretical physics from the University of Cambridge. He returned to Pakistan as a professor of mathematics in 1951–54 and then went back to Cambridge as a lecturer in mathematics. He became professor of theoretical physics at the Imperial College of Science and Technology, London, in 1957. Salam was the first Pakistani and the first Muslim scientist to win a Nobel Prize. In 1964 he helped found the International Centre for Theoretical Physics at Trieste, Italy, in order to provide support for physicists from Third World countries. He served as the centre's director until his death.

Salam carried out his Nobel Prize–winning research at the Imperial College of Science and Technology in the 1960s. His hypothetical equations, which demonstrated an underlying relationship between the electromagnetic force and the weak nuclear force, postulated that the weak force must be transmitted by hitherto-undiscovered particles known as weak vector bosons, or W and Z bosons. Weinberg and Glashow reached a similar conclusion using a different line of reasoning. The existence of the W and Z bosons was eventually verified in 1983 by researchers using particle accelerators at CERN.

EMILIO SEGRÈ

(b. Feb. 1, 1905, Tivoli, Italy—d. April 22, 1989, Lafayette, Calif., U.S.)

Italian-born American physicist Emilio Gino Segrè was cowinner, with Owen Chamberlain of the United States, of the Nobel Prize for Physics in 1959 for the discovery of the antiproton, an antiparticle having the same mass as a proton but opposite in electrical charge.

Segrè initially began studies in engineering at the University of Rome in 1922 but later studied under Enrico Fermi and received his doctorate in physics in 1928. In 1932 Segrè was appointed assistant professor of physics at the University of Rome. Two years later he participated in neutron experiments directed by Fermi, in which many elements, including uranium, were bombarded with neutrons, and elements heavier than uranium were created. In 1935 they discovered slow neutrons, which have properties important to the operation of nuclear reactors.

Segrè left Rome in 1936 to become director of the physics laboratory at the University of Palermo. One year later he discovered technetium, the first man-made element not found in nature. While visiting California in 1938, Segrè was dismissed from the University of Palermo by the Fascist government, so he remained in the United States as a research associate at the University of California, Berkeley. Continuing his research, he and his associates discovered the element astatine in 1940, and later, with another group, he discovered the isotope plutonium-239, which he found to be fissionable, much like uranium-235. Plutonium-239 was used in the first atomic bomb and in the bomb dropped on Nagasaki.

From 1943 to 1946 Segrè was a group leader at the Los Alamos Scientific Laboratory, Los Alamos, N.M. He was naturalized as a U.S. citizen in 1944 and was professor of physics at Berkeley (1946–72). In 1955, using the new bevatron particle accelerator, Segrè and Chamberlain produced and identified antiprotons and thus set the stage for the discovery of many additional antiparticles. He was appointed professor of nuclear physics at the University of Rome in 1974. He wrote several books, including

Experimental Nuclear Physics (1953), *Nuclei and Particles* (1964), *Enrico Fermi: Physicist* (1970), and two books on the history of physics, *From X-rays to Quarks: Modern Physicists and Their Discoveries* (1980) and *From Falling Bodies to Radio Waves* (1984).

ROBERT JEMISON VAN DE GRAAFF

(b. Dec. 20, 1901, Tuscaloosa, Ala., U.S.—d. Jan. 16, 1967, Boston, Mass.)

American physicist Robert Jemison Van de Graaff was the inventor of the Van de Graaff generator, a type of high-voltage electrostatic generator that serves as a type of particle accelerator. This device has found widespread use not only in atomic research but also in medicine and industry.

After working for a time as an engineer with the Alabama Power Company, Van de Graaff went to Paris in 1924 to study at the Sorbonne. There the lectures of Marie Curie turned his interests to atomic physics, and the following year he went to the University of Oxford to do research in the laboratory of the Irish physicist J.S.E. Townsend. While at Oxford, Van de Graaff was impressed with the need for a source of energetic beams of subatomic particles for the study of atomic behaviour. He conceived the idea for the Van de Graaff generator and, upon returning to the United States in 1929, continued to develop it.

Van de Graaff built his first generator in the early 1930s. The device, which is used for producing an exceptionally high electrostatic potential, depends for its operation on deposition of a charge on a moving belt of insulating fabric. This charge is conveyed on the belt into a smooth, spherical, well-insulated metal shell, where it is removed, passing to the metal shell. The shell increases in potential until an electric breakdown occurs or until the load current balances the charging rate. Machines of this kind, properly enclosed, have produced potentials of about 13,000,000 volts (13 megavolts). In a related device called the Pelletron accelerator, the moving belt is replaced by a moving chain of metallic beads separated by insulating material. The Pelletron accelerator at the Oak Ridge National Laboratory, Tenn., produces 25 megavolts and will accelerate protons or heavy ions, which are then injected into an isochronous cyclotron for further acceleration.

Van de Graaff became a research associate in 1931 and an associate professor in 1934 at the Massachusetts Institute of Technology (MIT), Cambridge. In 1946 he cofounded the High Voltage Engineering Corporation (HVEC) to manufacture his accelerator, and in 1960 he left MIT to work full time for HVEC.

ERNEST THOMAS SINTON WALTON

(b. Oct. 6, 1903, Dungarvan, County Waterford, Ire.—d. June 25, 1995, Belfast, N.Ire.)

Ernest Thomas Sinton Walton was an Irish physicist and corecipient, with Sir John Douglas Cockcroft of England, of the 1951 Nobel Prize for Physics for the development of the first nuclear particle accelerator, known as the Cockcroft-Walton generator.

After studying at the Methodist College, Belfast, and graduating in mathematics and experimental science from Trinity College, Dublin (1926), Walton went in 1927 to Trinity College, Cambridge, where he was to work with Cockcroft in the Cavendish Laboratory under Lord Rutherford until 1934. In 1928 he attempted two methods of high-energy particle acceleration. Both failed, mainly because the available power sources could not generate the necessary energies, but his methods were later developed and used in the betatron and the linear accelerator. Then in 1929 Cockcroft and Walton devised an accelerator that generated large numbers of particles at lower energies. With this device in 1932 they disintegrated lithium nuclei with protons, the first artificial nuclear reaction not using radioactive substances.

After gaining his Ph.D. at Cambridge, Walton returned to Trinity College, Dublin, in 1934, where he remained as a fellow for the next 40 years and a fellow emeritus thereafter. He was Erasmus Smith professor of natural and experimental philosophy from 1946 to 1974 and chairman of the School of Cosmic Physics at the Dublin Institute for Advanced Studies after 1952.

STEVEN WEINBERG
(b. May 3, 1933, New York, N.Y., U.S.)

American nuclear physicist Steven Weinberg in 1979 shared the Nobel Prize for Physics with Sheldon Lee Glashow and Abdus Salam for work in formulating the electroweak theory, which explains the unity of electromagnetism with the weak nuclear force.

Weinberg and Glashow were members of the same classes at the Bronx High School of Science, New York City (1950), and Cornell University (1954). Weinberg went from Cornell to the Nordic Institute for Theoretical Atomic Physics in Copenhagen for a year and then obtained his doctorate at Princeton University in 1957.

Weinberg proposed his version of the electroweak theory in 1967. Electromagnetism and the weak force were both known to operate by the interchange of subatomic particles. Electromagnetism can operate at potentially infinite distances by means of massless particles called photons, while the weak force operates only at subatomic distances by means of massive particles called bosons. Weinberg was able to show that despite their apparent dissimilarities, photons and bosons are actually members of the same family of particles. His work, along with that of Glashow and Salam, made it possible to predict the outcome of new experiments in which elementary particles are made to impinge on one another. An important series of experiments in 1982–83 found strong evidence for the W and Z particles predicted by these scientists' electroweak theory.

Weinberg conducted research at Columbia University and at the Lawrence Berkeley Laboratory before joining the faculty of the University of California at Berkeley in 1960. During part of his last two years there, 1968–69, he was visiting professor at the Massachusetts Institute of Technology. He joined its faculty in 1969, moving to Harvard University in 1973 and to the University of Texas at Austin in 1983.

FRANK WILCZEK

(b. May 15, 1951, New York, N.Y., U.S.)

American physicist Frank Wilczek, with David J. Gross and H. David Politzer, was awarded the Nobel Prize for Physics in 2004 for discoveries regarding the strong force—the nuclear force that binds together quarks (the smallest building blocks of matter) and holds together the nucleus of the atom.

After graduating from the University of Chicago (B.S., 1970), Wilczek studied under Gross at Princeton University, earning an M.S. in mathematics (1972) and a Ph.D. in physics (1974). He later served on the faculty at Princeton (1974–81) and taught at the University of California, Santa Barbara (1980–88). In 1989 Wilczek became a professor at the Institute for Advanced Study in

Frank Wilczek was one of three physicists who discovered that as the distance between two quarks increased, so did the force between them—much like a stretched rubber band—which led to the discovery of quantum chromodynamics (QCD). Rodrigo Buendia/AFP/Getty Images

Princeton, N.J., a post he held until 2000, when he moved to the Massachusetts Institute of Technology.

In the early 1970s Wilczek and Gross used particle accelerators to study quarks and the force that acts on them. The two scientists—and Politzer working independently—observed that quarks were so tightly bound together that they could not be separated as individual particles but that the closer quarks approached one another, the weaker the strong force became. When quarks were brought very close together, the force was so weak that the quarks acted almost as if they were free particles not bound together by any force. When the distance between two quarks increased, however, the force became greater—an effect analogous to the stretching of a rubber band. The discovery of this phenomenon, known as asymptotic freedom, led to a completely new physical theory, quantum chromodynamics (QCD), to describe the strong force. QCD put the finishing touches on the standard model of particle physics, which describes the fundamental particles in nature and how they interact with one another.

Wilczek also contributed to the study of questions relating to cosmology, condensed matter physics, and black holes. He was the recipient of numerous awards, including a MacArthur Foundation fellowship (1982).

EDWARD WITTEN

(b. Aug. 26, 1951, Baltimore, Md., U.S.)

American mathematical physicist Edward Witten was awarded the Fields Medal in 1990 for his work in superstring theory. He also received the Dirac Medal from the International Centre for Theoretical Physics (1985).

Witten was educated at Brandeis University (B.A., 1971) in Waltham, Mass., and Princeton University (M.A., 1974; Ph.D., 1976) in New Jersey. He held a fellowship at Harvard University (1976–77), was a junior fellow in the Harvard Society of Fellows (1977–80), and held a MacArthur Foundation fellowship (1982). He held an appointment at Princeton (1980–87) before moving to the Institute for Advanced Study, Princeton, in 1987.

Witten was awarded the Fields Medal at the International Congress of Mathematicians in Kyōto, Japan, in 1990. His early research interests were in electromagnetism, but he soon developed an interest in what is now known as superstring theory in mathematical physics. He made significant contributions to Morse theory, supersymmetry, and knot theory. Additionally, he explored the relationship between quantum field theory and the differential topology of manifolds of two and three dimensions. With the physicist Nathan Seiberg he produced a family of partial differential equations that greatly simplified Simon Donaldson's approach to the classification of four-dimensional manifolds.

Witten's publications include, with Sam B. Treimen, Roman Jackiw, and Bruno Zumino, *Current Algebra and Anomalies* (1985) and, with Michael B. Green and John H. Schwarz, *Superstring Theory* (1987).

CHEN NING YANG

(b. Sept. 22, 1922, Hofei, Anhwei, China)

Chen Ning (Frank) Yang was a Chinese-born American theoretical physicist whose research with Tsung-Dao Lee showed that parity—the symmetry between physical phenomena occurring in right-handed and left-handed coordinate systems—is violated when certain elementary particles decay. Until this discovery it had been assumed by physicists that parity symmetry is as universal a law as the conservation of energy or electric charge. This and other studies in particle physics earned Yang and Lee the Nobel Prize for Physics for 1957.

Yang's father, Yang Ko-chuen (also known as Yang Wu-chih), was a professor of mathematics at Tsinghua University, near Peking. While still young, Yang read the autobiography of Benjamin Franklin and adopted "Franklin" as his first name. After graduation from the Southwest Associated University, in K'unming, he took his B.Sc. in 1942 and his M.S. in 1944. On a fellowship, he studied in the United States, enrolling at the University of Chicago in 1946. He took his Ph.D. in nuclear physics with Edward Teller and then remained in Chicago for a year as an assistant to Enrico Fermi, the physicist who was probably the most influential in Yang's scientific development. Lee had also come to Chicago on a fellowship, and the two men began the collaboration that led eventually to their Nobel Prize work on parity. In 1949 Yang went to the Institute for Advanced Study in Princeton, N.J., and became a professor there in 1955. He became a U.S. citizen in 1964.

Almost from his earliest days as a physicist, Yang had made significant contributions to the theory of the weak interactions—the forces long thought to cause elementary particles to disintegrate. (The strong forces that hold nuclei together and the electromagnetic forces that are responsible for chemical reactions are parity-conserving. Because these are the dominant forces in most physical processes, parity conservation appeared to be a valid physical law, and few physicists before 1955 questioned it.) By 1953 it was recognized that there was a fundamental paradox in this field since one of the newly discovered mesons—the so-called K meson—seemed to exhibit decay modes into configurations of differing parity. Since it was believed that parity had to be conserved, this led to a severe paradox.

After exploring every conceivable alternative, Lee and Yang were forced to examine the experimental foundations of parity conservation itself. They discovered, in early 1956, that, contrary to what had been assumed, there was no experimental evidence against parity nonconservation in the weak interactions. The experiments that had been done, it turned out, simply had no bearing on the question. They suggested a set of experiments that would settle the matter, and, when these were carried out by several groups over the next year, large parity-violating effects were discovered. In addition, the experiments also showed that the symmetry between particle and antiparticle, known as charge conjugation symmetry, is also broken by the weak decays.

In addition to his work on weak interactions, Yang, in collaboration with Lee and others, carried out important work in statistical mechanics—the study of systems with large numbers of particles—and later investigated the nature of elementary particle reactions at extremely high energies. From 1965 Yang was Albert Einstein professor at the Institute of Science, State University of New York at Stony Brook, Long Island. During the 1970s he was a member of the board of Rockefeller University and the American Association for the Advancement of Science and, from 1978, of the Salk Institute for Biological Studies, San Diego. He was also on the board of Ben-Gurion University, Beersheba, Israel. He received the Einstein Award in 1957 and the Rumford Prize in 1980. In 1986 he received the Liberty Award and the National Medal of Science.

YUKAWA HIDEKI

(b. Jan. 23, 1907, Tokyo, Japan—d. Sept. 8, 1981, Kyōto)

Japanese physicist Yukawa Hideki was the recipient of the 1949 Nobel Prize for Physics for research on the theory of elementary particles.

Yukawa graduated from Kyōto Imperial University (now Kyōto University) in 1929 and became a lecturer there. In 1933 he moved to Ōsaka Imperial University (now Ōsaka University), where he earned his doctorate in 1938. He rejoined Kyōto Imperial University as a professor of theoretical physics (1939–50), held faculty appointments at the Institute for Advanced Study in Princeton, N.J. (U.S.), and at Columbia University in New York City, and became director of the Research Institute for Fundamental Physics in Kyōto (1953–70).

In 1935, while a lecturer at Ōsaka Imperial University, Yukawa proposed a new theory of nuclear forces in which

Yukawa Hideki at Columbia University, 1949. Encyclopædia Britannica, Inc.

he predicted the existence of mesons, or particles that have masses between those of the electron and the proton. The discovery of one type of meson among cosmic rays by American physicists in 1937 suddenly established Yukawa's fame as the founder of meson theory, which later became an important part of nuclear and high-energy physics. After devoting himself to the development of meson theory, he started work in 1947 on a more comprehensive theory of elementary particles based on his idea of the so-called nonlocal field.

The various topics in this section give some idea of the breadth of the field of particle physics. Subjects under consideration include the gas at the centre of white dwarf stars and the use of a diffracted beam of neutrons.

DEGENERATE GAS

The degenerate gas is a particular configuration, usually reached at high densities, of a gas composed of subatomic particles with half-integral intrinsic angular momentum (spin). Such particles are called fermions, because their microscopic behaviour is regulated by a set of quantum mechanical rules — Fermi-Dirac statistics. These rules state, in particular, that there can be only one fermion occupying each quantum-mechanical state of a system. As particle density is increased, the additional fermions are forced to occupy states of higher and higher energy, because the lower-energy states have all been progressively filled. This process of gradually filling in the higher-energy states increases the pressure of the fermion gas, termed degeneracy pressure. A fermion gas in which all the energy states below a critical value (designated Fermi energy) are filled is called a fully degenerate, or zero-temperature, fermion gas. Such particles as electrons, protons, neutrons, and neutrinos are all fermions and obey Fermi-Dirac statistics. The electron gas in ordinary metals and in the interior of white dwarf stars constitute two examples of a degenerate electron gas.

FERMI-DIRAC STATISTICS

In quantum mechanics, Fermi-Dirac statistics is one of two possible ways in which a system of indistinguishable particles can be distributed among a set of energy states: each of the available discrete states can be occupied by only one particle. This exclusiveness accounts for the electron structure of atoms, in which electrons remain in separate states rather than collapsing into a common state, and for some aspects of electrical conductivity. The theory of this statistical behaviour was developed (1926–27) by the physicists Enrico Fermi and P.A.M. Dirac, who recognized that a collection of identical and indistinguishable particles can be distributed in this way among a series of discrete (quantized) states.

In contrast to the Bose-Einstein statistics, the Fermi-Dirac statistics apply only to those types of particles that obey the restriction known as the Pauli exclusion principle. Such particles are named fermions, after the statistics that correctly describe their behaviour. Fermi-Dirac statistics apply, for example, to electrons, protons, and neutrons.

HYPERON

A hyperon is a quasi-stable member of a class of subatomic particles known as baryons that are composed of three quarks. More massive than their more familiar baryon cousins, the nucleons (protons and neutrons), hyperons are distinct from them in that they contain one or more strange quarks. Hyperons, in order of increasing mass, include the lambda-zero (Λ°) particle, a triplet of sigma (Σ) particles, a doublet of xi (Ξ) particles, and the omega-minus (ff) particle. Each of the seven particles, detected during the period 1947–64, also has a corresponding antiparticle.

The discovery of the omega-minus hyperon was suggested by the Eightfold Way of classifying hadrons, the more-general group of subatomic particles to which hyperons are assigned. Hadrons are composed of quarks and interact with one another via the strong force.

Hyperons are produced by the strong force in the time it takes for a particle traveling at nearly the speed of light to cross the diameter of a subatomic particle, but their decay by the weak force (which is involved in radioactive decay) takes millions of millions of times longer. Because of this behaviour, hyperons—along with K-mesons, with which they are often produced—were named strange particles. This behaviour has since been ascribed to the weak decays of the specific quarks—also called strange—that they contain.

ISOSPIN

Isospin is a property that is characteristic of families of related subatomic particles differing principally in the values of their electric charge. The families of similar particles are known as isospin multiplets: two-particle families are called doublets, three-particle families are called triplets, and so on.

The component particles of atomic nuclei, the neutron and proton, form an isospin doublet, since they appear to differ in nothing but electric charge and subsidiary properties. They are commonly thought of as different versions, or charge states, of the same object, called a nucleon. The isospin of a nucleon has a value of one-half. Isospin values are found by subtracting one from the number of members in its multiplet and then dividing by two.

The main importance of isospin in physics is that, when particles collide or decay under the influence of the strong nuclear force, their isospin is conserved. That is to say, even as the particles rearrange themselves or change into new particles, their total isospin value, computed in a specified way from the individual values, remains constant. Rules like this and others applicable to isospin (known as isospin selection rules) help physicists to consolidate their understanding of fundamental laws.

J/PSI PARTICLE

The J/psi particle is a type of meson consisting of a charmed quark and a charmed antiquark. It has a mass of 3.1 GeV/c², which is about 3.5 times larger than the mass of a proton. The particle was first detected in 1974 by two groups of American physicists working independently of each other, one headed by Burton Richter at SLAC (Stanford Linear Accelerator Center) in Menlo Park, Calif., and another headed by Samuel Ting at the Brookhaven National Laboratory in Upton, Long Island, N.Y. The discovery of the J/psi shed new light on quarks and their interactions. It provided support for the theory that there existed a fourth quark, called the charmed quark, in addition to those predicted by early quark models (i.e., the up, down, and strange quarks).

NEUTRON OPTICS

Neutron optics is the branch of physics dealing with the theory and applications of the wave behaviour of neutrons, the electrically neutral subatomic particles that are present in all atomic nuclei except those of ordinary hydrogen. Neutron optics involves studying the interactions of matter with a beam of free neutrons, much as spectroscopy represents the interaction of matter with electromagnetic radiation. There are two major sources of free neutrons for neutron-beam production: (1) the neutrons emitted in fission reactions at nuclear reactors and (2) the neutrons released in particle-accelerator collisions of proton beams with targets of heavy atoms, such as tantalum. When a neutron beam is directed onto a sample of matter, the neutrons can be reflected, scattered, or diffracted, depending on the composition and structure of the sample and on the properties of the neutron beam. All three of these processes have been exploited in the development of analytic methods, with important applications in physics, chemistry, biology, and materials science. Among the diverse achievements in the field of neutron optics, neutron-scattering studies have yielded insight into the fundamental nature of magnetism, probed the detailed structure of proteins embedded in cell membranes, and provided a tool for examining stress and strain in jet engines.

In contrast to fast neutrons, which act more exclusively as particles when they strike materials, slow, or "thermal," neutrons have longer wavelengths—about 10^{-10} metre, comparable in scale to the distance between atoms in crystals—and thus exhibit wavelike behaviour in their interactions with matter. Slow neutrons scattered by the atoms in a solid undergo mutual interference (similar to the behaviour of X-rays and light) to form diffraction patterns from which details of crystal structure and magnetic properties of solids can be deduced. The American physicist Clifford G. Shull and the Canadian physicist Bertram N. Brockhouse shared the 1994 Nobel Prize for Physics for their development of the complementary techniques and applications of neutron diffraction (elastic scattering) and neutron spectroscopy (inelastic scattering).

RENORMALIZATION

Renormalization is the procedure in quantum field theory by which divergent parts of a calculation, leading to non-sensical infinite results, are absorbed by redefinition into a few measurable quantities, so yielding finite answers.

Quantum field theory, which is used to calculate the effects of fundamental forces at the quantum level, began with quantum electrodynamics, the quantum theory of the electromagnetic force. Initially it seemed that the theory led to infinite results. For example, the electron's ability constantly to emit and reabsorb "virtual" photons (i.e., photons that exist only for the time allowed by the uncertainty principle) means that its total energy and its mass are infinite. However, by redefining the mass of the "bare" electron to include these virtual processes and setting it equal to the measured mass—that is, by renormalizing—the problem is removed.

Quantum electrodynamics has been the prototype for other quantum field theories. In particular, the highly successful electroweak theory, which incorporates the weak force together with the electromagnetic force, has proved to be renormalizable. Also, quantum chromodynamics, the theory of the strong force, appears to be renormalizable. However, a renormalizable theory that includes all the fundamental forces, in particular gravity, remains elusive.

GLOSSARY

annihilation In physics, a reaction in which a particle and its antiparticle (antimatter) collide and disappear.

atom Smallest unit into which matter can be divided and still retain the characteristic properties of an element.

boson Subatomic particle with integral spin that is governed by Bose-Einstein statistics.

charm In particle physics, the property or internal quantum number of the charm quark that is conserved in strong and electromagnetic interactions, but not in weak interactions.

collimate To render parallel to a certain line or direction.

electron Lightest electrically charged subatomic particle known.

electroweak theory Theory that describes both the electromagnetic force and the weak force.

fermion Any of a group of subatomic particles having odd half-integral spin (e.g., $\frac{1}{2}$, $\frac{3}{2}$).

Feynman diagram Graphical method of representing the interactions of elementary particles.

gauge symmetry Indicates that particular changes can be made without affecting the field's basic construction and means that the pertinent physical laws are the same in different regions of space and time.

gluon So-called messenger particle of the strong nuclear force, which binds quarks within the protons and neutrons of stable matter as well as within heavier, short-lived particles created at high energies.

hadron Any of the subatomic particles that are built from quarks and thus interact via the strong force.

isospin Property characteristic of families of related subatomic particles differing mainly in the values of their electric charge.

lepton Any member of a class of fermions that respond only to electromagnetic, weak, and gravitational forces and do not take part in strong interactions.

meson Any member of a family of subatomic particles composed of a quark and an antiquark.

neutrino Fundamental particle with no electric charge, little mass, and a spin value of ½.

neutron One of the constituent particles of every atomic nucleus except ordinary hydrogen.

oscillate To move back and forth, like a pendulum.

Pauli exclusion principle Assertion proposed by Wolfgang Pauli that no two electrons in an atom can be in the same state or configuration at the same time.

photon Minute energy packet of electromagnetic radiation.

positron Subatomic particle having the same mass as an electron but with an electric charge of +1 (an electron has a charge of 1).

proton Stable subatomic particle (one of the baryons) with a unit of positive electric charge and a mass 1,836 times that of the electron.

quark Any of a group of subatomic particles thought to be among the fundamental constituents of matter—more specifically, of protons and neutrons.

spin Amount of angular momentum associated with a subatomic particle or nucleus.

strong force Fundamental force acting between
elementary particles of matter, mainly quarks.
weak force Fundamental interaction that underlies
some forms of radioactivity and certain interactions
between subatomic particles.
Z particle Electrically neutral carrier of the weak force
and the neutral partner of the electrically charged W
particle.

BIBLIOGRAPHY

BOOKS FOR THE NONPHYSICIST

Frank Close, Michael Marten, and Christine Sutton, *The Particle Odyssey* (2002), is a full-colour illustrated guide to developments and discoveries in particle physics from 1895 to the beginning of the 21st century. Barry Parker, *Search for a Supertheory: From Atoms to Superstrings* (1987), describes the search for a unified theory of the fundamental forces and elementary particles. Leon M. Lederman and David N. Schramm, *From Quarks to the Cosmos: Tools of Discovery* (1989), is an illustrated account of modern particle physics and cosmology that links the small and large scales in the universe. Gordon Fraser, Egil Lillestøl, and Inge Sellevåg, *The Search for Infinity: Solving the Mysteries of the Universe* (1994), is a beautifully illustrated tour from the smallest particles of matter to the vast expanses of the universe. Gordon Kane, *The Particle Garden: Our Universe as Understood by Particle Physicists* (1995), describes how particle physicists have come to understand underlying laws of the universe and where future developments may lie. Gordon Fraser, *The Quark Machines* (1997), tells the story of the transatlantic "race" for discoveries in particle physics, with emphasis on the role of CERN. Gerard 't Hooft, *In Search of the Ultimate Building Blocks* (1997), is a Nobel laureate's firsthand account of particle physics from the 1960s to the 1990s.

TEXTBOOKS

Jonathan Allday, *Quarks, Leptons, and the Big Bang* (1998), is an introductory textbook aimed at high-school students with no previous knowledge of particle physics. G.D. Coughlan and J.E. Dodd, *The Ideas of Particle Physics: An Introduction for Scientists* (1994), bridges the gap between popular accounts and detailed textbooks for readers with some background in the physical sciences. Robert N. Cahn and Gerson Goldhaber, *The Experimental Foundations of Particle Physics* (1991), a more-technical introductory text, is a collection of important papers on discoveries in particle physics, together with commentary aimed at physics students.

HISTORICAL ACCOUNTS

Abraham Pais, *Inward Bound: Of Matter and Forces in the Physical World* (1986), is a detailed scholarly account of major developments in subatomic physics, in particular from 1895 to the 1960s. Laurie M. Brown and Lillian Hoddeson (eds.), *The Birth of Particle Physics* (1983); Laurie M. Brown, Max Dresden, Lillian Hoddeson, and May West (eds.), *Pions to Quarks* (1989); and Lillian Hoddeson, Laurie M. Brown, Michael Riordan, and Max Dresden (eds.), *The Rise of the Standard Model* (1997), are three books based on symposia held to consider developments during three major eras in the history of particle physics, from the 1930s to the 1990s, with many firsthand accounts from the scientists involved. Lochlainn O'Raifeartaigh, *The Dawning of Gauge Theory* (1997), is a study of the development of gauge theory, with commentary on important papers in the field. Gordon Fraser (ed.), *The Particle Century* (1998), is a collection of essays highlighting the major developments in particle physics, including firsthand accounts from Nobel Prize winners. An interesting collection of important papers on electroweak theory is contained in C.H. Lai (ed.), *Selected Papers on Gauge Theory of Weak and Electromagnetic Interactions* (1981).

PARTICLE ACCELERATORS

Discussions of modern accelerator designs can be found in three articles from *Scientific American*: John R. Rees, "The Stanford Linear Collider," 261(4):58–65 (October 1989); Stephen Myers and Emilio Picasso, "The LEP Collider," 263(1):54–61 (July 1990); and Leon M. Lederman, "The Tevatron," 264(3):48–55 (March 1991). Also useful are Andrew M. Sessler, "Gamma-Ray Colliders and Muon Colliders," *Physics Today*, 51(3):48–53 (March 1998); and Justin Mullins, "Perfect Pitch," *New Scientist*, 159(2144):52–53 (July 25, 1998). An extensive survey for nonspecialists is available in the article "Particle Accelerator," in *McGraw-Hill Encyclopedia of Science & Technology*, 8th ed., vol. 13, pp. 126–155 (1997).

More-technical works include Philip J. Bryant and Kjell Johnsen, *The Principles of Circular Accelerators and Storage Rings* (1993); D.A. Edwards and M.J. Syphers, *An Introduction to the Physics of High Energy Accelerators* (1993); *AIP Conference Proceedings* (irregular), papers from seminars and courses published by the American Institute of Physics; and *IEEE Transactions on Nuclear Science* (bimonthly), for new developments in accelerator technology.

Classic research papers of historical interest include J.D. Cockcroft and E.T.S. Walton, "Experiments with High Velocity Positive Ions," *Proceedings of the Royal Society of London, Series A*, vol. 137, pp. 229–242 (1932), on the cascade generator; and a selection of articles in

Physical Review: Robert J. Van De Graaff, "A 1,500,000 Volt Electrostatic Generator," 38:1919–20 (1931); D.W. Kerst, "Acceleration of Electrons by Magnetic Induction," 60:47–53 (1941), on the betatron; Ernest O. Lawrence and M. Stanley Livingston, "The Production of High Speed Light Ions Without the Use of High Voltages," 40:19–35 (1932), on the classical cyclotron; David H. Sloan and Ernest O. Lawrence, "The Production of Heavy High Speed Ions Without the Use of High Voltages," 38:2021–32 (1931), on the development of the linear resonance accelerator idea; Edwin M. McMillan, "The Synchrotron: A Proposed High Energy Particle Accelerator," 68:143–144 (1945); and papers in Claudio Pellegrini and Andrew M. Sessler (eds.), *The Development of Colliders* (1995).

INDEX

quantum electrodynamics (QED),
18, 20, 23, 25, 28, 49–52, 53,
63–64, 68, 71, 73, 162
quark-gluon plasma, 92–94, 148
quarks, 1, 5, 6, 7, 10, 11, 13, 14,
20, 23–24, 25, 29, 32, 33, 36,
38, 39, 40, 42, 44–48, 55, 62,
63, 64, 66, 72, 78, 79, 80, 81,
82, 85, 86, 87, 92, 93, 94, 95,
96, 97, 98, 102, 157, 158, 159,
160, 161, 163, 164, 172, 173,
175, 176, 183, 184, 191, 192
quark theory, development of,
59–64

R

radioactive isotopes, 43
Reines, Frederick, 35, 161
Relativistic Heavy Ion Collider
(RHIC), 94, 148
renormalization, 52, 73, 77
resonance, 38, 45, 59, 60
Richter, Burton, 40, 161
Rochester, George, 56
Rubbia, Carlo, 79, 153, 181, 184–185
Rubin, Vera, 90
Rutherford, Ernest, 3, 41, 49, 52,
115–116, 167, 189

S

Salam, Abdus, 75, 76, 78, 171, 172,
181, 185–186, 190, 191
Scherk, Joel, 101
Schwartz, Melvin, 35
Schwarz, John, 98, 101–102
Schwinger, Julian, 52
Seaborg, Glenn T., 180

sector-focused cyclotrons,
128–129
Segrè, Emilio, 10, 168, 186–188
Serber, Robert, 54
size, and subatomic particles,
4–5
Sloan, David H., 116
Snyder, H. S., 118
Soddy, Frederick, 3
special relativity, theory of, 8, 9,
37, 50–51, 83
spin, 6–8, 10, 14, 17, 21, 24, 26, 29,
30, 33, 39, 45, 46, 50, 53, 55,
56, 57, 59, 61, 62, 70, 71, 75, 83,
84, 86, 87, 97, 98, 158, 162, 163
Stanford Linear Accelerator
Center (SLAC), 33, 84, 131,
160–162
Stanford Linear Collider, 132,
161, 162
Standard Model, 2, 7–8, 39, 41,
48, 72, 81–82, 85, 87, 92, 95,
97, 153, 154, 156, 184, 193
Steinberger, Jack, 35
strangeness, 57, 61, 72, 93
string theory, 98, 99–106, 173, 182
strong force, 13, 20, 23–25, 27, 29,
30, 36, 37–38, 42, 47, 56, 61,
63, 64, 66, 69, 81, 84, 94, 95,
96, 97, 99, 100, 101, 157, 163,
172, 173, 183, 184, 191, 192
Sudbury Neutrino Observatory
(SNO), 36, 88
supergravity, 83, 84, 98
Super-Kamiokande detector, 89
supersymmetry, testing, 82–87
Susskind, Leonard, 100
SU(3) symmetry, 44, 57–59, 61,
63, 64

Y

Z